Here is a bracing, memorable and deeply encouraging exposition of the Bible's teaching on the subject of God's work in the world and our part in it. I warmly commend this volume to those who have persevered in Christian service for many years, and to those newly dipping their toes into the privileges and responsibilities of being stewards of the gospel, heralds of the excellencies of the Saviour and labourers in the Lord's harvest field.

Kanishka Raffel, Dean of St Andrew's Cathedral, Sydney.

This outstanding book provides a magnificent overview of what it means to be a Christian disciple in service of the Lord Jesus. It is full of pithy, practical, challenging, and most importantly, Biblical insight. I have benefited personally from reading it, and I intend to recommend it to many others.

William Taylor, Rector of St Helens, Bishopsgate, London.

LATIMER BRIEFING 22

MINISTRY UNDER THE MICROSCOPE

The What, Why, and How of Christian Ministry

ALLAN CHAPPLE

The Latimer Trust

ISBN 958-1-906327-51-4

Cover photo: "Close up of examining of test sample under the microscope in laboratory." © by kkolosov – fotolia.com

Scripture quotations are from the New International Version, copyright © 2011 and the New American Standard Bible, copyright © 1995. Used by permission. All rights reserved.

Published by the Latimer Trust February 2018

The Latimer Trust (formerly Latimer House, Oxford) is a conservative Evangelical research organisation within the Church of England, whose main aim is to promote the history and theology of Anglicanism as understood by those in the Reformed tradition. Interested readers are welcome to consult its website for further details of its many activities.

The Latimer Trust
London N14 4PS UK
Registered Charity: 1084337
Company Number: 4104465
Web: www.latimertrust.org
E-mail: administrator@latimertrust.org

Dedicated
with gratitude and affection
to the two men whose ministries have taught me most

Paul Barnett and Peter Adam

generous and encouraging friends
steadfast servants of the Lord Jesus

CONTENTS

PREFACE

I have never been completely sure what a Preface is for—but it seems like a good place to express my thanks to...

Allison	While I think and read and write about Christian ministry, she just gets on and does it, to the benefit of many people – and not least me, for forty-four years so far!
George Frederic Handel	For the huge amount of stunningly good music that makes me look forward to more time at my writing desk!
Derek Jones	For noticing what my first attempt at the "Ministry Map" had omitted – and for long lasting friendship.
Kanishka Raffel	For the kind words about this book – and for all that he gave me for fifteen years as my pastor-teacher, not least his warm friendship.
Grace Raven	For all the painstaking work she has done to bring the book into print.
William Taylor	For the kind words about this book – and for many others the only time we have met.
The members of the Christian community that is Trinity Theological College	For continuing to model what this book is about, in large ways and small, because it is much easier to write about what I am seeing and experiencing every day than about merely abstract ideas.
Most of all, the God of all grace	For delivering me totally and forever from all that I deserve into a glorious and endless salvation I will never deserve; for the winder of the lavish love that is never to be withdrawn despite betrayals without number; and for the amazing kindness that still entrusts me with the privilege of serving even though my best efforts are deeply flawed!

INTRODUCTION

You may well be wondering, "Is this the book for me?" If so, this Introduction will help you to work out the answer by dealing with the main questions you are likely to be asking about the book.

What is this book about?

This question is not ignoring the title of the book but asking what the key word "ministry" means. You are probably familiar with it as a word often used in church circles—and that has been the case for a long time. When I became a Christian in the 1960s, it was common to speak about people "going into the ministry" or becoming a "minister". This referred to those who were ordained by their denomination and appointed to be the pastor-leader of one of its churches. Catholics had "priests" and Protestants had "ministers". Later on it became more common to drop "the" and just use "ministry" as a label for what people like pastors or youth workers did. Such people were sometimes distinguished from other believers as those who were "in full-time ministry". The basic reason we have used the word in such ways is that our English Bibles had used it for a very long time—and that has given us something of a problem.

For centuries, before William Tyndale and others translated the Bible into English in the sixteenth century, the Bible of Christendom was in Latin. As a result, many Latin words made their way into the English language. That is how we got the words "ministry" and "minister", whose Latin equivalents mean "service" and "servant". So when the Greek New Testament was being translated into English, it was not surprising that the "ministry" words were used for "service" words in Greek. Those who produced the famous King James Version of 1611 saw no reason to change this decision, which meant that generations of English speakers became accustomed to using "ministry" and related words to refer to important features of church life. Those responsible for the Revised Version of 1881 and the Revised Standard Version of 1952 largely retained these words because the longstanding use of the King James Version meant that they were widely used and well known.

11

The unfortunate result of all this was that where the Greek New Testament was speaking about the serving that we should all do because we are all servants, our English Bibles seemed to be telling us about the ministry of those who were ministers—and these words had long since come to refer to the special role that only a few of us have. Our Bibles referred to Paul and his colleagues as "ministers" (e.g., 2 Cor 3:6; 1 Tim 4:6), and to the apostles as having a "ministry of the word" (Acts 6:4)—and the nearest equivalent we had to this was pastors and what they did. That is how the church-words I became familiar with as a new Christian had become established.

So does its title mean that this book is about what the people we used to call "ministers" do? What they do is certainly included—but what we are putting under the microscope is "service", which is what all Christians should be doing all the time. That immediately raises another question: why do we need to put serving "under the microscope"? We have seen that the way it has been used in our Bibles has given the word lots of special nuances, like barnacles on the hull of an old ship and we need to scrape them off to get back to the timbers underneath! In other words, we need a clear understanding of what the Bible means by "service". Since everyone who belongs to the Lord Jesus is a servant, it is essential that we know what that means, so that we can all be what we should be and do what we should do.

The way we will put it "under the microscope" is to make a careful examination of what the Bible teaches us—that is, what God teaches us— about Christian service. It should be more obvious than it often seems to be that the Bible is the primary and most important ministry manual we have—something that John Calvin saw clearly:

> Woe to the slothfulness of those who do not peruse the oracles of the Spirit day and night to learn from them how to discharge their office.[1]

---

[1]   John Calvin, Calvin's New Testament Commentaries (Eerdmans, 1964 [1548]), 10.247 [on 1 Tim 4:13].

That is why the rest of this book keeps referring you to passages in the Bible.[2] Please don't ignore them! It is really important that you look them up and read them carefully. This applies especially to anything in the book that is new to you or that differs from what you have been taught before, for you must not simply take my word for it. My ideas are no foundation on which to build your ministry! Everything about the way we serve the Lord should be governed by what he says to us in Scripture. It is absolutely essential that our work for God is faithful to the word of God.

Who is this book for?

Since "ministry" does not mean "what ministers do" but the serving that all believers should be doing, I hope the book will be of some help to every Christian. But I have written it to help some Christians in particular: those who are often said to be "in full-time ministry".

Before we continue, I need to explain why you won't find that expression in this book. There are two reasons why I believe we should stop using it. The first has to do with what it implies. If we describe a few of us in this way, we can only mean that the rest of us are "in part-time ministry"—but it is simply not possible to be a part-time servant of the Lord Jesus! If I serve him only some of the time, who am I serving the rest of the time? Since "no one can serve two masters" (Matt 6:24), choosing to be a part-time servant of Jesus would have to mean choosing not to be his servant at all.

My second reason for not using "full-time ministry" is that it isn't what the Bible tells us. Look at what Paul says to Christian slaves in Colossae when he is teaching them about how they should live. He does not tell them to serve their masters faithfully, and when (if?) they get time off to attend Christian meetings they might then get an opportunity to serve the Lord. What he does say is very different: by serving their masters faithfully, they are actually "working for the Lord" (Col 3:23). They do not need to get time off so that they can serve the Lord once in a while: "it is the Lord Christ you

---

2   The Bible translation I am usually referring to is the NIV2011, but sometimes you will find the letters NASB after a reference to a particular passage. This means that I am referring to the 1995 edition of the New American Standard Bible.

are serving" (Col 3:24)—and Paul means that this is true all the time! This is a very different view of "full-time ministry" from the one that people usually express.

We can now return to the question of who this book is for. If we can't say "those who are in full-time service", how do we specify which Christians it is meant to help? Unfortunately, we have a bit of a problem here, as there is no generally agreed way of referring to the people I have in mind. Some speak of "those in vocational ministry". This is OK if our hearers take "vocation" to mean my occupation: what I am employed to do—but if they know that it originally concerned what God calls all of us to be and do, we still have a problem, because "ministry" is every believer's "vocation". Others prefer to speak of "those in word-ministry". Again, this can work if we use it with care—but it risks downplaying or overlooking the fact that there is a sense in which all believers should serve in this way. Within the church-family, our calling is to speak the truth to each other in love and wisdom: truth that flows from and leads back to the gospel, the "word of Christ" (Eph 4:15; Col 3:16). We are also to have such a "ministry of the word" to outsiders, with words full of grace that explain our hope in Christ (Col 4:6; 1 Pet 3:15-16). This ministry is exercised in the home by parents to their children and by the host to the members of a home group Bible study, or exercised weekly in the coffee-shop by the Christian who reads the Bible with a new believer or an interested inquirer. So those who are said to be "in word-ministry" differ from the rest of us only because this is their primary focus and responsibility, not because it is a responsibility that belongs only to them.

The "least worst" way of saying it that I can think of is to refer to those who hold a "ministry position" or a "ministry appointment"—by which I mean the people in a church who have a designated leadership role to which the church has appointed them and for which they are usually paid: pastors, youth workers, and the like. Although I think this book will be helpful to others as well—such as elders and other unpaid leaders in a local church—it is intended to benefit two groups in particular: those who are wondering whether they should be serving in a ministry position and those who already hold one. Talking about Christian ministry from this perspective means that we won't be focusing on how the rest of us are meant to serve the Lord Jesus in our homes, our workplaces, and our communities, as well as in our churches. Some of what we learn will apply to these areas of service, but if you are looking for a book with that focus, this one won't give you all that you need.

Why "ministry" and not "leadership"?

By investigating Christian ministry from the perspective of those who hold ministry positions, we will be discussing Christian leadership—so why isn't the book called "Leadership under the Microscope"? While I wouldn't object to that title, there are two things that have held me back from using it. The first is that it is not uncommon for leadership to be seen in rather grandiose terms, even amongst Christians. If someone is referred to as a "church leader", this is often taken to mean that they are the church equivalent of a business organisation's CEO. And while there may be some overlap between such a role and that of the senior pastor of a large church, there should be some very fundamental differences between them. It is because I think "leadership" is in danger of diluting or even eclipsing those differences that I have decided to stick with "ministry"—despite the barnacles we have noted! But it is important not to run away from that fact that holding a ministry position makes me a leader. So even if I am not the senior pastor of a mega-church but the youth worker in an ordinary-sized church, I will not discharge my ministry faithfully if I fail to lead as I should. My service in this role must have being a good leader at its core.

My second reason for not using "leadership" in the title of the book is that I think there is a serious risk in doing so. No, I don't mean that Christian books should not use this word in their title! Since every church and every Christian organisation needs good leadership, we need helpful books on leadership like those included in the Bibliography at the end of this book. The risk I am referring to is treating leadership as primary, equal in importance to serving, instead of recognizing that it is a form of service—a very important form, but no more than that. Why does this matter? What is at stake here? The difference between these two approaches can be put this way: the church of God is not distinctive because it has an unusual approach to leadership, expecting its leaders to behave as servants. It is distinctive because all of its members are servants, and some of them serve by leading. Ministry is foundational: serving is the root and leadership is no more than one of its fruits. This means that before we can give our attention to leadership we must first ensure that we have a good grasp of what the Bible teaches us about Christian service—and that is what this book is all about.

What help will this book give me?

There are two ways in which I think it will be helpful. The first has to do with its focus and aim. There are lots of good books about particular kinds of service, but it is surprisingly difficult to find any that set out to answer the fundamental question, "What is Christian ministry?" And that is what this book seeks to do. So it is not a "how to" book: it doesn't teach you such things as how to lead a Bible study group or write a sermon or run an evangelism course or do hospital visits—not because these aren't important, but because they can only be done as they should be when they are seen in the right context and from the right perspective. In other words, know-what and know-why are more basic and more necessary than know-how! If we do not have a clear biblical grasp of what ministry is and why God calls us to do it, our ministry can all too easily end up as little more than shrewd pragmatism—or to put it more bluntly, clever worldliness—when it should be displaying consistent and deep-seated faithfulness to the Lord and his word. It is essential that what we believe about ministry and what we do in ministry is determined not by our own ideas and desires, or by the agenda of the world around us, but by the character and purpose of God. If we are to do his will, we must be governed by his word.

The second benefit of this book has to do with the way it answers the big question about the nature of Christian ministry. It does not try to cover everything, but seeks to identify and explain the fundamental elements of what the Bible tells us. In other words, it is meant to give you a big-picture view of Christian ministry: what I like to call a "ministry map". My reason for doing this is that maps are very useful! And there are two situations in particular where they prove their worth.

When you go somewhere new, it is a helpful to look at a map before you get there. It is easier to find your way around if you have some idea of the layout of your new location. So if you are trying to work out whether the best way for you to serve the Lord is in a ministry position, a ministry map will give you a good idea of what that looks like.

A map is also very useful if you are lost—and it is not uncommon for people in ministry positions to end up feeling lost and confused. One of the main reasons this happens is that they have never had a ministry map. So when they entered new territory by taking up a ministry position, they had no clear idea of what they were getting into and have struggled to find their way. If that is how you feel about your ministry, the ministry map this book gives you will help you to work out where you are and how to get to where you should be.

The first thing you will find after you have finished this Introduction is the Ministry Map. This is my attempt to summarize what the Bible teaches us about Christian ministry and to set it out in a way that shows the connections between its various aspects. The rest of the book is divided into four sections that correspond to the four main points of the map. In each section we will work through the relevant part of the map point-by-point, with what the Bible teaches about each point covered in no more than a few pages. Each of these Bible studies concludes with about four or five quotations "worth pondering", which means what it says: whether or not we end up agreeing with them, thinking about what they say will pay dividends. They are drawn from works published in the sixteenth century by the Reformers and their immediate successors through to works published in our own day.

As you read through the book, you will find a certain amount of repetition in it, with some topics being covered in several places and some points being made more than once—sometimes even in the same words. I think this is a strength rather than a weakness, because what we are investigating is more like a large spider's web than a large set of pigeonholes. We cannot get a clear grasp of what the Bible teaches us about Christian ministry by working through a list of separate topics. Instead, we need to examine the fundamental ingredients from a number of different angles, observing all the ways in which they are linked together and interact with each other.

The way the book is organised means that it can be used in various ways: you can read right through it as with any other book; you can work through it one point at a time; you can use it like a manual, looking up the relevant sections as you need them. But no matter how you end up using it, it is important to remember that it is not meant to be your final destination. It should be nothing more than a stepping-stone that takes you into the Bible, so that God's words nourish, strengthen, direct, equip, warn, correct, and focus you in all the ways that are needed if your ministry is to be what it should be.

I hope this answer has helped you to work out whether this book is for you. If not, you may well have friends who could find it helpful and would appreciate being told about it. No, this is not a thinly-disguised attempt to sell more copies of the book! There is a great need everywhere for more people to take up ministry positions, and for those who have done so to be supported and encouraged in what can be difficult and even lonely work—and if this book helps even just a few people in these ways, I will be more than satisfied!

THE MINISTRY MAP

CHRISTIAN MINISTRY IS...

1. **grounded ...**

    1.1. on Jesus the Servant-Lord

        1.1.1. he is the pioneer of ministry: we must be served by him
    - he came into the world to serve and save those who are lost forever without him
    - he gave up everything in serving and saving us—so now we belong to him and must serve him

        1.1.2. he is the pattern for ministry: we must serve like him
    - this must be humble, like his foot-washing
    - this must be sacrificial, like his suffering and dying

    1.2. on God's grace and truth

        1.2.1. on his grace

        1.2.2. on his truth

        1.2.3. so our ministries must be full of grace and truth

2. **determined by God's work**

    2.1. God is at work, bringing in his salvation and establishing his kingdom

        2.1.1. he does this by his Spirit and with his word

        2.1.2. we must do God's work in God's way
    - we must rely on the Holy Spirit
    - we must practice responsible dependence, working hard and taking initiatives for the sake of God's gospel and kingdom
    - his word must be the focus and the foundation of our ministries
        - (a) we must keep holding it fast
            - we must never alter it
            - we must never abandon it
        - (b) we must keep making it known
            - widely throughout the world
            - deeply throughout the church

2.2. God includes us in the work he is doing

    2.2.1. God does not need anything we can do for him

    2.2.2. yet he gives us a place in his work, conferring on us the great dignity of being his co-workers

    2.2.3. so all ministry is a privilege, a gift from a gracious God

2.3. Our work is framed by God's work

    2.3.1. we serve between the comings of Jesus: his past completed work and his future completing work

    2.3.2. so Christian ministry is tough
- because of our enemies—the world, the flesh, the devil—and all the ways in which they tempt or threaten us
- because of our many weaknesses
- because of our sinfulness
- because of the sins of others
- in the New Testament, the three greatest areas of failure are truth (false teaching), love (division), and holiness (immorality)

    2.3.3. so Christian workers must be accountable
- we should be accountable to our fellow-believers
- we are accountable primarily to the Lord, who will judge our ministries

    2.3.4. so Christian ministry is glorious
- God gives us the privilege of being his coworkers in "the work of the Lord"
- this work cannot fail
- its fruit will be eternal and glorious

3. dependent on God's gifts

3.1. God equips us to serve him

3.2. There are many different ministry gifts

3.2.1. all are important and all are necessary, yet no one has all the gifts

3.2.2. so we serve together: Christian ministry is collaborative
- hence all of the "co-" words in Paul's letters
- hence all of the colleagues he names in his letters
- so leadership in the local church is shared

3.3. There are two main types of service

3.3.1. some ministries are more basic than others, hence the "some for all" pattern of ministry

4. focused ...

4.1. on God's Son

4.1.1. he is our message

4.1.2. our ministries are from him and also for him

4.2. on God's work

4.2.1. mission: winning the world

4.2.2. maturity: growing the church

4.2.3. majesty: displaying his glory

4.3. on some essential commitments

4.3.1. prayer

4.3.2. the "ministry of the word"

4.3.3. loving God's people

4.3.4. setting a godly example

4.3.5. persevering through hardships

4.4. on some crucial tasks

4.4.1. evangelism: winning the lost

4.4.2. discipling: establishing and equipping believers

4.4.3. caring for the flock, especially the most needy

4.4.4. training new workers

4.5. on God's glory

    4.5.1. we must not be self-seeking, engaged in self-promotion

    4.5.2. we should do everything for God's glory

    4.5.3. we must not glory in our gifts or ministries but in God himself

Part 1: THE BASIS OF CHRISTIAN MINISTRY

1. Christian ministry is grounded ...

1.1. on Jesus the Servant-Lord

1.1.1. he is the pioneer of ministry: we must be served by him

We must receive what he did when he came into the world to serve and save us, since we are lost forever without him. By his death for us he has bought us and made us his own—so now we belong to him and should live for him.[1]

Where should we begin when we want to understand Christian ministry? Not, as we might have expected, with ourselves: our gifts, our calling, our duties. Instead, we must begin with the Lord Jesus. That is because everything about Christian ministry is defined by who he is and what he has done, and is doing, and will do. It is from him that we learn what serving—which is what "ministry" means—is all about.

This becomes clear if we start with the question, "Why did Jesus come into the world?" The Bible gives several major answers to this question, one of the most important coming from Jesus himself (Matt 20:28; Mark 10:45). When we look carefully at what he says here, we discover four crucial truths he wanted his disciples to grasp.

The first is that he had come to "serve". The way he says so acknowledges that this would have been quite a shock: "*even* the Son of Man ..." They knew by then that this common way in which Jesus referred to himself was connected with a mysterious figure Daniel had seen in a vision. What that vision tells us is that God gave this "son of man" such glory and sovereignty that everyone on earth worshipped him (Dan 7:13-14). By making him greater than anyone else is or could be, God clearly intended that he would receive the honour that would normally be given only to God himself. So the very last thing anyone could have expected is that this supreme and exalted sovereign would occupy the lowest rung on the ladder as a mere servant. But that is exactly what Jesus wanted his disciples to know about him: although higher than anyone else could

---

[1]   Acts 20:28; Rom 14:7-9; 1 Cor 6:19-20; 7:22-23; 2 Cor 5:14-15; Tit 2:14; Rev 5:9.

possibly be—sovereign over all and to be worshipped by all—he has put himself in the lowest place of all. And this is not a terrible mistake on his part; it is why he had come.

This leads us to the second point Jesus was making. He had already told the disciples that he was going to be killed in Jerusalem.[2] But he wanted to make sure that they would see this the right way: his life would not be taken from him, for he was going to "give" it.[3] That is what he had come to do. It was important that the disciples knew that he had come to serve, but it was even more important that they knew that this is the kind of a servant he had come to be. He would go as far down as it was possible to go—all the way down to death. And this would not be forced upon him; it was the path he chose to take, the service he gave freely. But why would someone so great choose to go down so very low? What could be the point of such sacrifice?

This is where we see the third point in what Jesus said. From one perspective, he was going to die because of what the Jewish leaders and their Roman rulers would do to him. And there was nothing noble about this death when it came: he died on a cross—the most shameful and degrading death anyone could die, which the Romans deliberately reserved for people they regarded as utterly contemptible. But that is only the outside of the story. Jesus would appear to be just a passive victim, when in reality he was going to be doing something immensely important for our benefit. This is the inside of the story: he was going to give himself up to death as our "ransom". This means that he would redeem us by dying for us, paying the price that freed us from our captivity to sin and death.[4] So the death that would look like a crushing defeat would actually be a mighty act of rescue, saving us from our terrible lostness. And this was going to be big: he would be saving not just a few but a great "many".

Since we have now come to the end of this verse, where do we find the fourth point? It becomes clear when we recall that Jesus made the

---

2   Mark 8:31; 9:12, 31; 10:33-34.
3   John 10:17-18; Gal 1:4; 2:20; Eph 5:2, 25; Tit 2:14.
4   Rom 3:24-25; 8:1-3; Gal 3:13; 4:4-5; Eph 1:7; Col 1:14; 1 Tim 2:6; Tit 2:14; Heb 9:12, 15; 1 Pet 1:18-19; Rev 1:5.

first three points in response to his disciples' competitive scramble for prestige. The way he is going to serve tells them that they must live as servants—and it shows them how to do so: his service gives us both an obligation we must accept and also a pattern we must follow (Matt 20:25-27; Mark 10:42-44). But this is not what comes first. What Jesus says about his service means that it is unique—so there is an important sense in which we cannot serve like him. His service saves us—and it is the only service that could do so. Only he—and no one else—could give his life to ransom us, to release us from our dreadful bondage. If we are to serve we must first be saved—so before we can serve him we must let him serve us. We must receive him as our redeemer before we can follow him as our example.

Because Jesus has served us by going to death as our ransom, we are the comprehensively saved and deeply loved children of the Father.[5] We come to know God in this way only when we accept what Jesus has done to serve and save us. Unless we do so, admitting that we desperately need to be rescued and cannot do anything to save ourselves, we gain no benefit from this totally undeserved work of humble, self-sacrificing service. That is a crucial lesson Peter had to learn: unless he allowed his Lord to go down very low and serve him, he could not belong to him (John 13:8). Peter could only be his if he accepted his service. Like Peter, we all need a Saviour—so we must be willing to have Jesus as our Servant. And that is where all ministry begins: not with us serving him, but with him serving us. So Christian ministry can only be done by the converted, that is, by those who have turned away from their sins, believed the gospel, and given their loyalty to Jesus as Lord and Saviour. There is not much point in reading on unless you have done so!

Jesus our Servant-Saviour is also our Lord. Because of the way he served us, we are now owned by him. The ransom-price he paid to set us free was also the purchase-price he paid to make us his: by his death he bought us and made us his own. So he is now our Master and we are his slaves, bound to serve him.[6] Yet this is not a burdensome duty but a great

---

[5]   Gal 4:4-7; Eph 1:3-14; Col 1:18-22; 2:13-15; 2 Tim 1:9-12; Tit 3:4-7.
[6]   Luke 12:35-38, 42-44; 17:7-10; John 13:16; 15:20; Rom 1:1; 12:11; 14:18; 16:18; 1 Cor 3:5; 4:1; 7:22-23; Gal 1:10; Phil 1:1; Col 3:24; 4:12; 2 Tim 2:24; Jas 1:1; 2 Pet 1:1; Jude 1; Rev 1:1; 2:20.

privilege, not a harsh imposition laid upon us but a response of grateful love drawn from us. We are the joyful servants of Jesus the Servant, the willing slaves of Jesus the Lord. Because he died for us, we now live for him (2 Cor 5:15), determined to make our lives count for the self-giving, sin-bearing Saviour to whom we now belong.

All of this tells us something crucial about Christian ministry: that it is not an initiative we take for the Lord but a response we make to him. What he does for us comes first, both in time and in importance. What we do for him is our answer to the service by which he saves us. We do not put him in our debt by serving him! Rather, we serve him because we have an incalculable debt to him. We give ourselves to him because he gave himself for us. Just as we love him because he first loved us (1 John 4:19), so too we serve him because he first served us. Jesus the Servant-Lord is the pioneer of ministry.

Worth pondering ...

When we appreciate Christ as our redeemer-rescuer and his great love in dying for us, we nail our rights to his cross. With gratitude, we hand our lives and our gifts to him and commit ourselves unreservedly to his service. Leadership begins at the foot of the cross.[7]

The race is not to the top, where the power and prestige are. The race, for followers of Jesus, is to the bottom where humility, surrender and service are to be found.[8]

In the Kingdom of God, service is not a stepping stone to nobility; it is nobility, the only kind of nobility that is recognised.[9]

He hath given himself wholly for us; left heaven for us; denied himself for us; made himself of no reputation for us; became ... a curse for us. And in way of requital we should answer him, with giving ourselves and all we have to him... we must not live to ourselves as our own, but give ourselves to him, and not to anything else; we are not our own, nor man's, but the Lord's.[10]

No ministry is worth anything at all which is not first and last and all the time a ministry beneath the Cross.[11]

---

7   Chua Wee Hian, Learning to Lead: Biblical Leadership Then and Now (IVP, 1987), 18.
8   Brian J. Dodd, Empowered Church Leadership: Ministry in the Spirit according to Paul (IVP, 2003), 142.
9   T.W. Manson, The Church's Ministry (Hodder & Stoughton, 1948), 27.
10 Richard Sibbes, Works, 7 volumes (Banner of Truth, 1977 [1639]), 5.305, 311.
11 James Stewart, Heralds of God (Hodder & Stoughton, 1946), 200.

1. Christian ministry is grounded ...

1.1. on Jesus the Servant-Lord

1.1.2. he is the pattern for ministry: we must serve like him

We must be like him in his footwashing: we must serve humbly.[12] And we must be like him in his suffering: we must serve sacrificially.[13]

Ministry begins with the Lord Jesus. He came to serve us—and he did so by going all the way down to terrible death as our ransom. By serving us in this way he has rescued us, setting us free and making us his. Admitting our need for his service and receiving the salvation it gives us is where we begin: this must be our introduction to ministry. So there are some important ways in which his service differs from ours: it comes first as the foundation of our service, and it does what ours could never do. Jesus the Servant is the only Saviour of the world—and the only Saviour it could ever have.[14]

Once we have begun with Jesus the Servant-Lord and understood how his service is very different from ours, we can then take the next step. This is where we see two important connections between his service and ours. It is from his service that we learn both that we are to serve and also how we are to serve. Jesus made this clear to his disciples with the "for" that begins Mark 10:45. It is because he had come to serve—even though, as the Son of Man, he is supreme and sovereign over all—that they should be servants and not rulers, slaves and not lords (Mark 10:42-44). His "not so with you" is for us as well as for them, of course. His service, and especially its climax—giving up his life to ransom us from terrible bondage—gives us both a motive and a model for our service.

It will be obvious to everyone who understands what he has done in serving and saving us that the only fitting response to such amazing grace

---

[12] John 13:14-17; Phil 2:3-8; 1 Pet 5:3-6.
[13] John 12:24-26; 1 Cor 4:9-13; 9:19, 27; 15:30-32; 2 Cor 1:3-9; 6:3-10; 11:23-29; 12:10, 15; Eph 3:13; Phil 1:29-30; 2:29-30; Col 1:24; 1 Thess 2:9; 2 Tim 1:8; 2:3, 8-10; 3:10-11; 4:5.
[14] John 4:42; Acts 4:12; 1 John 4:14.

is for us to serve him. As we have seen, he is the pioneer of ministry: he surrendered everything to save us—so we must now give everything we are and have to serve him. We learn how to do so by considering the way he has served us. In Jesus we see the pattern of ministry: he is our model as well as our Master (John 13:13-15). This means that we serve him by following him: by going on ahead of us, he has carved out the path we must now take.

The Bible tells us many things about the path on which we follow Jesus the Servant. It is the path of obedience. As it did for him, for us too it means choosing to do the will of God instead of following our own desires (Mark 14:21, 36; Phil 2:8). It is the path of love where, like him, we choose to give ourselves for the sake of others (Gal 2:20; Eph 5:1-2). It is also the path of humble service. This is such an essential part of our lives that Jesus did something dramatic and unexpected to make sure his disciples saw the point and never forgot it. On what would be his last night with them, he took on the most menial task of the lowest servant by washing their feet (John 13:1-5). He then made it clear that they must see this as an example they should follow (John 13:12-17). So we must rid ourselves of any sense of dignity or importance that would keep us from serving. And we must not regard any task as beneath us. Instead, we must keep growing down in humility, recognizing that our highest calling and greatest dignity is to be servants of Jesus, the Servant-Lord.[15]

Since this must be at the heart of our discipleship, it must also characterise every aspect of our ministries, especially our leadership. It is crucial to see this the right way. Christian leadership is not benevolent rule but responsible service. It is not that we are leaders who take an unusual approach to leadership, choosing to lead by serving. What we are is servants—servants of Jesus who have been entrusted with the privilege of serving his people by leading them. This does not mean that they follow us: they are servants of Jesus, and so they follow him. That is why we lead them: so that they keep following him with an ever-growing love for him, loyalty to him, and likeness to him. That is how our leadership

---

[15] Luke 12:35-38, 42-44; 17:7-10; John 13:16; 15:20; Rom 1:1; 12:11; 14:18; 16:18; 1 Cor 3:5; 4:1; 7:22-23; Gal 1:10; Phil 1:1; Col 3:24; 4:12; 2 Tim 2:24; Jas 1:1; 2 Pet 1:1; Jude 1; Rev 1:1; 2:20.

serves his glory and their good. The church of God is not a strange organisation whose leaders are expected to serve; it is a family made up of servants, some of whom are entrusted with the privilege of leadership.

Following Jesus along the pathway of service also means making sacrifices and facing suffering. We see his sacrifice in what he was prepared to give up and also in what he was prepared to go through. The Bible tells us that he let go of unimaginable riches and made himself a pauper for us (2 Cor 8:9). He left the highest possible position in order to go all the way down to the lowest possible place (Phil 2:6-8). He went from the throne to the cross and the tomb, from eternal glory to terrible shame and disgrace. He went from being sinless to bearing sin for us (2 Cor 5:21)—and thus from the intense joy of unbroken fellowship with his Father to the dreadful darkness of separation from him and judgment at his hands. In these and many other ways, the sacrifices he made and the sufferings he endured go far, far beyond anything we could ever face. In all of this he was doing what only he could do—and yet he was also pioneering the path we must take (Heb 12:1-3). Our approach to ministry must reflect both of these facts.

The path that Jesus took for us meant the cross—and that is our calling too.[16] This is the path we must choose every day (Luke 9:23). By sacrificing himself for us, he not only saved us, he also claimed us. His death was both the ransom-price that set us free and also the purchase-price that made us his—so we now belong to him. And as he gave his life for us, so we are to yield our lives to him, holding nothing back for his sake and the gospel's (Mark 8:35). We must be ready, for his sake, to suffer abuse and scorn, danger and loss, threats and violence, and even death.[17] We are to be like him in his sacrifice (Phil 2:5-8) and like him in his suffering (1 Pet 2:21).

While everyone who belongs to Jesus must follow him on this path, there is a sense in which sacrifice and suffering especially mark those

---

[16] Matt 10:38; 16:24; Mark 8:34; Luke 14:27.
[17] Matt 5:10-12; Luke 6:22-23; John 15:18-20; 16:1-4; Acts 8:1-3; Phil 1:27-30; 1 Thess 2:14; 3:2-4; 2 Thess 1:4-7; Heb 10:32-34; 12:3-11; 1 Pet 2:20-23; 3:14- 17; 5:8-9; Rev 2:2-3, 9-10, 13; 6:9-11.

who hold ministry positions.[18] Ministry is no easy option, a safe haven for people looking for prestige and power. The world might do it this way, but serving Jesus gives us a very different agenda. If serving us meant suffering for him, then that is what we should expect in our ministries, for the servant is not greater than the master (Matt 10:24; John 13:16). And since that is so, we must never think that sacrifice and suffering in our ministries make us heroes who deserve lots of praise. We must never forget that what the Lord Jesus gave up and went through for us is infinitely greater than any loss or pain that we might have to bear. In order to serve and save us, he was prepared to pay a price more terrible than we will ever be able to grasp. So how could we hold back if serving him means forgoing a few pleasures or receiving a few wounds?

In marked distinction from what is true in the world, Christian ministry does not focus on status or power. That is because it means serving the Lord who went all the way down so as to win for us a secure and eternal place in his great salvation. By doing so, he established the pattern that all ministry should follow. Like him, we are meant to give humble, sacrificial service.

If we are to stay true in our ministries, it is essential that we have a clear grasp of the first and most fundamental fact about Christian service. To make sure that we have got it, let us say it again. To understand ministry we must not begin by focusing on ourselves but on Jesus the Servant-Lord. Our ministries are the service we give as people who have been served and saved by him. That we serve him rests on the prior fact that he has served us—and the way we serve him responds to the way he has served us. Christian ministry is what it is because of our Lord Jesus Christ, who is both the pioneer and the pattern of ministry.

---

[18] Matt 10:16-25; Mark 10:28-30; Acts 5:40-41; 7:54-60; 9:22-30; 20:19, 23; 1 Cor 4:9-13; 2 Cor 6:3-10; 11:23-28; 1 Thess 2:2, 14-16; 2 Tim 1:8; 2:8-12; 3:10-12; 4:14-16.

Worth pondering ...

Can we behold him washing and wiping his servants' feet, and yet be proud and lordly still?[19]

If the eternal Son of God, your Savior and Lord, has not come to be served but to serve others, if he has given his soul for you and the deliverance of many, if he stripped himself of the divine form ... [and] took the form of a servant, if he has become obedient to death, and the death on the cross, what then will you, O man, do with yourself? ... I will keep nothing for myself but with joy will put all I possess at the service of my brethren. I will also be obedient in death, even in the death of the cross; that is, I will accept all sufferings and disgrace. And so it will happen that we shall deny ourselves, put the cross on our shoulders and thus follow our Lord, Master, King and Savior, and certainly also like him pass from this life of humility, service and obedience into the eternal glory, kingdom and blessedness.[20]

[If] we want to be humble, we must move from looking at the life of Jesus to looking at the cross of Jesus. His life shows us humility; his cross humbles us... The secret of humility is never to stray far from the cross.[21]

Whatever our Master was pleased to condescend to in favour to us, we should much more condescend to in conformity to him. Christ, by humbling himself, has dignified humility, and put an honour upon it, and obliged his followers to think nothing below them but sin... When we see our Master serving, we cannot but see how ill it becomes us to be domineering.[22]

Since my Lord served me even though He was not obliged to do so, and since He sacrificed life and limb for me, why would I refuse to serve Him in return? He was completely pure and without sin. Yet, He humbled Himself so deeply, shed His blood for me, and died to blot out my sins. Ah, should I then not also suffer something because it pleases Him?[23]

---

[19] Richard Baxter, The Reformed Pastor (Banner of Truth, 1974 [1656]), 143.
[20] Martin Bucer in Graham Tomlin (ed), Philippians, Colossians, RCS: NT XI (IVP Academic, 2013), 47f.
[21] Tim Chester, The Ordinary Hero: Living the Cross and Resurrection (IVP, 2009), 36, 37.
[22] Matthew Henry, Commentary on the Whole Bible (Hendrickson, 2008 [1721]), 1603 [on John 13:16].
[23] Martin Luther, Works (Concordia, 1967 [1523]), 30.85 [on 1 Pet 2:21].

1. Christian ministry is grounded ...

1.2. on God's grace and truth

1.2.1. dependent on his grace

Just as the foundations determine the size and shape of any building, so Christian ministry is what it is because of its foundations. Its content and character are controlled by what it rests on, by where it is grounded. We have learned that everything about Christian ministry depends upon Jesus the Servant-Lord, the pioneer and pattern of ministry. The Bible also makes it clear that our ministries are meant to be determined at every point by God's grace and God's truth.

To have a clear understanding of what the first of these means, we need to know what the Bible means by "grace". The clearest indication we get comes from the way it is used alongside such words as "kindness", "love", and "mercy" (Eph 2:4-7; Tit 3:4-7), which shows that "grace" refers to God's way of loving us. The use of a special word implies what the New Testament spells out: that this love is unique—and there are two ways in which that is so. The first is that it is always free: God's love for us always comes as a gift and not a reward, because it is never deserved.[24] Secondly, it is always rich: it is always lavish and unstinting, never restrained or reserved.[25] God's grace is love that is never merited and never limited, always poured out on those who have no claim on it at all.

There is one place above all others where we see this grace, and that is the cross of Jesus: "God demonstrates his own love for us in this: while we were still sinners, Christ died for us" (Rom 5:8).[26] This remarkable love is found only in God ("his own love") and not in us. While "even sinners love those who love them" (Luke 6:32), God's cross-love is for those who were his enemies--and while "even sinners lend to sinners, expecting to be repaid in full" (Luke 6:34), God's cross-love makes utterly

---

[24] Rom 3:24; 5:15-17; Eph 1:6; 2:8; 2 Tim 1:9; 1 Pet 1:13.
[25] Rom 2:4; 5:15-17; Eph 1:7; 2:4, 7.
[26] See also Rom 3:24-25; 5:15-19; Eph 1:6-8a; 4:32–5:2; Heb 2:9; 1 John 3:16; 4:9 -10.

destitute wretches rich beyond our wildest dreams![27] In both respects, this love is simply stunning: it is exactly the opposite of what we deserve and should have expected, and it withholds nothing from us.[28]

How does God's amazing grace form the foundation of Christian ministry? The New Testament gives us four main answers to this question. First, our ministries are created by his grace. We have seen that what comes first is what he does for us: our service is not a noble initiative we take for him, but a glad and humble response to the love he has shown in serving and saving us. We serve because he first served us.

God's grace is basic in another sense as well, because our service is not what he needs from us but a gift he has given us (Acts 17:25; 2 Cor 4:1). We have a place in his service only because in his grace he makes room for us and includes us in what he is doing. We serve not in response to the harsh demand of a despot, nor as conscripts coming to the aid of a weak and needy ruler, but as the deeply loved children of a Father with infinite kindness and a Sovereign with infinite riches. So Christian ministry is a great privilege, the fruit of great grace. We see this very clearly in Paul, who never lost his sense of wonder at the grace that entrusted him with his apostolic ministry.[29] Although there are major differences between his ministry and ours, we should be filled with the same wonder and gratitude, keenly aware that our ministries too exist only because of the grace of God. We will examine this important fact more fully when we reach section 2.2 of the Ministry Map.

Secondly, our service is focused on the grace of God, for this is the content of the gospel (Acts 20:24; Col 1:5-6). The message we are to convey to a lost world is "the word of his grace" (Acts 14:3, NASB)—and this is also the message by which the church lives (Acts 20:32). Since God is "the God of all grace" (1 Pet 5:10) and the gospel is "the gospel of the grace of God" (Acts 20:24, NASB), grace should be the constant focus and principal theme of our ministries. Something has gone badly wrong if we cannot say of those who learn the gospel from us that they have "truly understood God's grace" (Col 1:6). While our conversation in

---

[27] Rom 5:10; 2 Cor 8:9; Eph 1:3, 7-8; 2:6-7; Col 1:21-22.
[28] See especially Psa 103:8-12; Rom 8:32.
[29] Rom 15:15; 1 Cor 3:10; 15:10; Eph 3:7-8; 1 Tim 1:12-14.

general should be "full of grace" (Col 4:6), those who hear our preaching and teaching should be hearing "words of grace" (Luke 4:22, literally). We can never draw their attention to God's grace too often or make it too important in their eyes.

Equally, we ourselves can never ponder it too deeply or delight in it too much—yet there is a danger here that we must not ignore. Sooner or later, anything we keep thinking or teaching about begins to feel obvious—so obvious that we take it for granted and stop thinking and speaking about it. So we will probably need to pray—privately for ourselves, and publicly for those we serve—that the Holy Spirit will keep us from ever reaching the point where we lose our sense of wonder and gratitude at the way God loves us. While there is not normally any particular reason when I wake up to thank God that the new day means another sunrise, the fact that it is also going to be one more day in which God loves me deeply and generously is a very good reason to thank him. If this isn't my regular practice, perhaps I need to work my way through the gospel again!

Thirdly, our ministries are enabled by God's grace. This is true in two ways. In his grace God gives us the gifts we need to serve him. The many different ways in which we serve are all expressions of the grace-gifts that he gives to each one of us.[30] And his grace is not only bountiful, it is also powerful. It is God's grace that empowers our service, giving us the strength we need to serve him.[31] Even our best efforts are incapable of yielding lasting fruit unless God is at work in us and with us—and this is one of the chief ways he displays his grace, shaping and empowering what we do for him. That is why Paul and others were entrusted to the grace of God for the work that had been assigned to them (Acts 14:26; 15:40)—and also why they reported back on what he had done through their ministry (Acts 14:27).

Christian ministry is, fourthly, to be nourished by God's grace. It is grace that provides the right motivation for our service: we serve the Lord because he has served us to make us his, and because he has made room for us in his work. The more we remember and reflect on the grace of

---

[30] Rom 12:6; Eph 4:7; 1 Pet 4:10.
[31] 1 Cor 15:10; 2 Cor 12:9-10; 2 Tim 2:1.

God, the greater our incentive for serving him—and doing so gladly and willingly. So this is not just a matter of what we teach others; it is also about what we preach to ourselves. If we must insist that no one can be justified by works of the law (Rom 3:20, 28; Gal 2:16), we must also insist that we cannot be justified by works of ministry! We need to keep reminding ourselves that the work that secures God's approval is not the work we do for him but the work he has already done for us. In the face of our relentless quest for acceptance and significance, the gospel of grace directs us away from ourselves to Another—and away from our flawed efforts to the glory of his comprehensive and completed work. When our ministries are anchored in the gospel, we do not serve for acceptance but from acceptance, and we find our significance not in our service but in our Saviour.

Worth pondering ...

Justification by faith keeps us from the need for self-justification, or the need always to be noticed or praised by others. As such, it is a powerful remedy to self-delusion and despair. If I am always dependent upon the assessment of others for approval ... chances are I will put my energies into work that will win the most approval and applause. In so doing, I will be failing to do the real work of pastoring, and even what real work of pastoring I do will be done from improper motives. Justification by faith will provide me with the glue that will enable me to stick to my real tasks, seeking the approval of the One who really counts.[32]

Oh, if ever you would have your souls kept low, dwell upon the free grace and love of God to you in Christ. Dwell upon the firstness of his love, dwell upon the freeness of his love, the greatness of his love, the fulness of his love, the unchangeableness of his love, the everlastingness of his love, and the activity of his love. If this do not humble thee, there is nothing on earth will do it.[33]

Grace transcends love.... It is love which ... has an unexhausted wealth of kindness. Grace transcends mercy. Mercy forgives sin, and rescues the sinner from eternal darkness and death. But grace floods with affection the sinner who has deserved anger and resentment, trusts penitent treachery with a confidence that could not have been merited by ages of incorruptible fidelity, confers on a race which had been in revolt honours which no loyalty could have purchased, on the sinful joy beyond the desert of saintliness.[34]

Not only should we actively battle for the gospel as the fundamental paradigm for every ministry of the church, but we must also fight for the gospel to be the resting place of our hearts... many [pastors] sadly function in a regular state of gospel amnesia. They forget to preach privately to themselves the gospel that they declare publicly to others. When you forget the gospel, you begin to seek from the situations, locations, and relationships of ministry what you have already been given in Christ. You begin to look to ministry for identity, security, hope, well-being, meaning, and purpose.[35]

---

32   Peter Brain, Going the Distance: How to Stay Fit for a Lifetime of Ministry (Matthias, 2004), 250.
33   Thomas Brooks, Works (Banner of Truth, 1980 [1661]), 3.37.
34   R.W. Dale, The Epistle to the Ephesians: Its Doctrine and Ethics, 6th ed. (Hodder & Stoughton, 1892), 178.
35   Paul David Tripp: Dangerous Calling: The Unique Challenges of Pastoral Ministry (IVP, 2012) 99.

1. Christian ministry is grounded ...

1.2. on God's grace and truth

1.2.2. governed by his truth

Ministry that has God's grace as its foundation will also be grounded on—and so governed by—God's truth. That is because the basis and focus of Christian ministry is the gospel, which the New Testament refers to as the "word of truth",[36] or simply as "the truth".[37] This reflects the fact that the gospel proclaimed by the apostles issued from the work of the "Spirit of truth".[38] He guided them into all the truth about Jesus, giving them both true understanding of who he is and what he has done for us and also the very words in which to communicate this truth (John 16:13; 1 Cor 2:12-13). So "the word of truth" means "the true word, the true message"—but it can also mean "the message about the truth". This too fits the gospel, because its subject is the Lord Jesus Christ, who brought the truth into the world, not only making it known but also embodying it as the only one among us who is completely and utterly true, the truth in person.[39] The gospel is thus the truth about the Truth!

While the New Testament often refers to the gospel as the truth, it also makes it clear that God's truth is not limited to the gospel message. A helpful way of understanding this is to think of the truth as a set of three concentric circles. At the centre is the Lord Jesus, who both reveals and embodies the truth. The circle surrounding him is the gospel, the word of truth. The outer circle contains the Old Testament Scriptures—and just as Jesus is the subject and focus of the gospel, so Jesus and his gospel is the subject and focus of the Scriptures.[40] And because God is the "God of truth", every one of his words is true and his word as a whole

---

[36] Eph 1:13, NASB; Col 1:5, NASB; 2 Tim 2:15; Jas 1:18.

[37] 2 Cor 4:2; Gal 2:5, 14; 5:7; Eph 4:21; 2 Thess 2:10, 12-13; 1 Tom 2:4; 4:3; 2 Tim 2:18, 25; 3:8; 4:4; Tit 1:1, 14; Heb 10:26; Jas 5:19; 1 Pet 1:22; 2 Pet 1:12; 1 John 2:21; 3:19; 2 John 1; 3 John 3, 8.

[38] John 14:17; 15:26; 16:13-14; 1 John 4:6; 5:6.

[39] John 1:14, 17; 8:31-32, 40, 45-46; 14:6; 18:37; 1 John 5:20; Rev 3:7, 14; 19:11.

[40] Mark 14:21, 27, 49; Luke 24:25-27, 44-47; John 5:39, 46; Acts 3:18-24; 10:43; 13:27-39; 17:2-3; Rom 1:1-4; 1 Pet 1:10-12.

is "right and true".[41] This also applies to the New Testament Scriptures, which result from the unique work of the "Spirit of truth" in and with the apostles.[42] A ministry grounded on the truth will therefore be governed by the Lord Jesus Christ, with the gospel and the Bible the means by which he rules his people.

The fact that Christian ministry is grounded on God's truth gives us both great confidence and great responsibility. This confidence results from the existence of the Bible, which means that God's truth is in the public domain in fixed and objective form. As a result, we all have access to his truth—and we all have access to the same truth, not to many subjective views all claiming to be from him. The Bible gives us the truth about God from God—which means that this is truth that never changes and never needs to change.

Since all of God's words are flawless (Psa 12:6; Prov 30:5), without defect or error of any kind, we can have complete confidence in the Bible, knowing that it will not mislead us. Yet while we can trust everything it teaches us, it does not teach us everything: although it is wholly true, it is not the whole truth. The Bible looks at this from two sides: one is the fact that God has not revealed everything to us (Deut 29:29)—but what we have is real revelation; the other is the fact that we know only in part (1 Cor 13:9)—but what we have is real knowledge. God has given us all the truth we need to know about his character and purpose and will: to know what he is like, and what he is doing, and how he wants us to live.

Having true knowledge of God enables us truly to know him, to live rightly with him and for him. This would not be possible if we did not have his truth. If we did not know what the Bible tells us, everything we believed would be nothing but guesswork that could never be verified. We would spend every day groping our way through life like people lost in a thick fog with no light, no map, and no compass. What a great mercy to be delivered from such misery by being called out of darkness into God's wonderful light (1 Pet 2:9)! And what a privilege to live in that light as children of light (Eph 5:8; 1 Thess 5:5)!

---

41   Psa 31:5, NASB; 33:4; 119:160; Isa 65:16, NASB.
42   See especially 1 Cor 2:12-13; 14:37; 1 Thess 4:1-3, 8; 2 Pet 3:2, 15-16.

Having God's truth in Scripture also enables us to serve him as we should. There is, in fact, no better or more important ministry manual than the Bible. This is one of the major ministry lessons Paul sets out in what proved to be his last letter (2 Tim 3:14-17). When he urges Timothy to continue in what he has learned (verse 14), the context makes two things clear. The first is that he is referring to Timothy's knowledge of the Scriptures (verse 15), and the second is that what he has learned from Scripture should continue to shape his ministry (4:1-5). Paul then reinforces this important principle by making three closely connected points (verses 16-17). First, he reminds Timothy of the unique character of Scripture as "God-breathed", as coming from the mouth of God. He then points out that this enables Scripture to do what we all need: to be taught, to have our errors pointed out and corrected, and to be trained for living the right way. Finally, he indicates that Scripture's ability to function in this way enables it to equip God's servant in a comprehensive way.

Paul is usually understood to be making this point: when Timothy gives people "careful instruction" from the Scriptures (4:2), this will do its work in their lives (verse 16b) and give them all they need to live as believers should (verse 17). While there is no doubt that Paul wanted this to happen, this is not what he is getting at. The servant of God in verse 17 is not the Christian believer but Timothy.[43] So Paul is not referring to the way Timothy will use the Scriptures to equip other believers for godly living; he is pointing out how the Scriptures will equip Timothy for effective ministry. When he continues in what he has learned, and when he keeps applying the Scriptures to himself, so that he is taught and corrected and trained, then his ministry will be shaped and directed by God's word in the way that it should be.

While it is a great privilege to know God's truth, this brings with it a very great responsibility. That is because the truth has to play two crucial and connected roles in our lives. The first results from the fact that every one of us needs to be saved. There is only one place where salvation is to

---

[43] The actual expression Paul uses is "the man of God". Since his only other use of it is in 1 Tim 6:11, where he is addressing Timothy, it is unlikely that he is using it in a different sense in this verse.

be found—and that is in the Lord Jesus, the only Saviour of the world; and there is only one bridge that gets us to him, only one means of believing in him—and that is the gospel, the message proclaimed by the apostles.[44] So we cannot be saved unless we believe and love this truth (2 Thess 2:10-13). But its work is not done at this point, for the new life we enter by believing it needs the kind of foundation and direction that only the truth can give. The gospel that leads us to Jesus also enables us to live in him.

The impression is sometimes given in Christian circles that the gospel is like the launch rocket that drops away once it has got the satellite into orbit, because its job is done and it has no further use. But the subject of the gospel is riches that are boundless (Eph 3:8), a gift too great for words to describe fully (2 Cor 9:15)—so we will never reach the point where we need more than the gospel can offer us. We do not grow as Christians by moving beyond the gospel or away from the gospel; we grow only by moving deeper into the gospel—just as a plant keeps growing upwards because its roots keep going down.

That is why Christian ministry has the gospel at its heart, why everyone who has any leadership role in a local church is in the truth business and must give priority to being a truth-teller. If people are to come to the Lord Jesus and then to live in him, we must keep making the gospel known, proclaiming and teaching the truth set out in Scripture. We must explain it so clearly that no one will misunderstand it—and make its great richness so obvious that no one can ever justify going elsewhere. And because it is God's word, God's truth, we have no right or reason to change it in any way. We must not distort it by adding to it or subtracting from it, but must set forth the truth plainly (2 Cor 4:2), confident that God will use it powerfully to advance his saving purpose in people's lives.

This kind of truth-telling is the heart of our responsibility—but it is not all that we must do. We will not be able to communicate the truth as clearly and deeply as we should unless we keep working hard to grow in our understanding of it. This is essential for another reason as well. Unless those we teach continue holding fast to the gospel, they will not

---

44   John 4:42; 17:20; Acts 4:12; 1 John 4:14.

THE BASIS OF CHRISTIAN MINISTRY

be saved—so for their sake we must be able to identify and expose false gospels and also to defend the gospel against the attacks of hostile critics.[45] And we must always be on guard so that we do not let ourselves drift away from the gospel or be lured away by seductive lies.[46] Being faithful in these ways is unlikely to make us popular, since it is not at all uncommon for people to stop listening to the truth, or to go one step further and reject it, or to go even further still and oppose it.[47] But we will not stop being its heralds and teachers (2 Tim 4:2), for we love the truth (2 Thess 2:10)—and that is because we love the One it is all about.

Our responsibility goes further than this, for it is not enough for the truth to be always in our minds and on our lips. The truth of the gospel is meant to govern the whole of our lives. That is why the Christian life is called the "way of truth" (2 Pet 2:2), for we should be people who "do the truth" and "walk in the truth".[48] We are to live worthily of the gospel (Phil 1:27), and that means living in line with the truth of the gospel (Gal 2:14). That is why the apostles teach both the word of God, the gospel, and the will of God, the way of life that arises from and meshes with the gospel.[49] We see this in their letters, which unpack the implications of the gospel by applying it to the whole range of needs and problems they had to address. So the content of their letters arises from the gospel, which is embedded at their core, more often than it articulates the gospel. The recipients of these letters are being taught about the new life that is the fruit of which the gospel is the root: the way of life required of all who believe the gospel, the truth that is in Jesus (Eph 4:17, 20-21). And we cannot urge those we teach to live like this unless they can see that we are doing so—which is why we must maintain the same close watch over our lives as we do over our doctrine (1 Tim 4:16). What is heard from me should also be seen in me (Phil 4:9).

---

45 Rom 16:17-18; Gal 1:6-8; 5:1-8; Phil 1:7, 16; 3:2-3, 18-19; Col 1:21-23; 2:8, 16- 19; Tit 1:9- 14; Jas 5:19-20; 1 John 2:24; 2 John 9; Rev 2:24-25; 3:3, 11.
46 1 Tim 1:18-19; 4:7, 15-16; 5:20-21; 2 Tim 1:13-14; 2:16, 23; Heb 2:1; 2 John 8-9.
47 2 Tim 3:8; 4:3-4; Tit 1:14.
48 John 3:21 (translated literally); 1 John 1:6 (translated literally); 2 John 4; 3 John 3-4.
49 Eph 4:20-24; Col 1:9-10; 2:2-3; 1 Thess 2:13; 4:1-3; 2 Thess 2:13-15; 3:6; 1 Tim 3:14-15; Tit 2:1-12; 1 John 2:7, 22-24; 3:11.

Worth pondering ...

> [The] true knowledge of Christ [is] if we receive him as he is offered by the Father: namely, clothed with his gospel. For just as he has been appointed as the goal of our faith, so we cannot take the right road to him unless the gospel goes before us.[50]

> [Those] who are called by God to preach his Word must be resolved that they will not compromise, even if the whole world were to rise up against them. They must bear all conflicts, knowing that God will help them in their need and always grant them victory, provided they follow their vocation in purity and simplicity. The greatest insult and injury that we can give to God is in yielding to the desires of man, and twisting his Word both left and right. It is not only a question of abandoning our own ideas, but also of constantly upholding God's truth, which is immutable; it must never be altered, however changeable and inconstant men may be.[51]

> Paul instructs Timothy to devote himself to preaching the Word (2 Tim. 4:2), precisely because that Word makes the man of God "adequate, equipped for every good work" (2 Tim. 3:17). Timothy didn't need the latest rhetorical techniques, business practices, or creative ministry models based on captivating metaphors. He simply needed to be guided, governed, and geared by the Word of God.[52]

> While it is helpful and necessary to think outside the box in terms of fresh and creative ways to communicate the gospel and to organise church, we must be those who avoid innovation at all costs when it comes to the message we proclaim... we are to take every step necessary to ensure that we neither add nor take away; we are simply stewards, guarding a deposit... Being a steward, of course, feels much less exciting and is much less prestigious than being an innovator. We won't steal headlines and attract the limelight by saying what has been said before... So we need to ask ourselves: in our own thinking and understanding and in our teaching and preaching, are we guarding the gospel deposit as humble stewards, or are we seeking the limelight as innovators?[53]

---

[50] John Calvin, Institutes of the Christian Religion, 2 volumes (SCM, 1960 [1559]), III.ii.6 [1.548].

[51] John Calvin, Sermons on Galatians (Banner of Truth, 1997 [1563]), 505.

[52] Mark Dever & Paul Alexander, The Deliberate Church: Building Your Ministry on the Gospel (Crossway, 2005), 21.

[53] Jonathan Griffiths, The Ministry Medical: A Health-Check from 2 Timothy (Christian Focus, 2013), 41-43.

1. Christian ministry is grounded on ...

1.2. God's grace and truth

1.2.3. so our ministries must be full of grace and truth

The Bible makes it clear that our lives and our ministries—like the Lord we love and serve (John 1:14, 17)—should be full of grace and truth. How can we ensure that this is the case? And how does being grace-full and truth-full work itself out in the day-to-day realities of ministry? We have answered these questions to some extent in the previous few pages—but since most of us are very slow to learn these things, it is worth taking another look and also going a bit deeper.

The first point we must make is that grace-full and truth-full ministries are the fruit of the gospel, which is God's word of truth about God's work of grace (Col 1:5-6, NASB). When I am grounded and centred on the gospel as I should be, this cannot fail to have a decisive and growing impact on the character of my ministry. One of the most important ways it will shape me is that love and truth will work together as partners instead of competing for supremacy as rivals.

This has often been a problem amongst Christians because of a widespread tendency to regard love and truth as alternatives rather than allies—a stance that is reinforced by the fact that our temperaments incline us to favour one over the other. This can make it seem as though there are two competing kinds of Christians, with those who believe we must give priority to love viewed by the others as soft on the truth, and those who insist we must hold fast to the truth often seen as hard-hearted and unloving. What we learn from the Bible should make us very uneasy about dividing love and truth like this, because of the way they are united in the Lord Jesus, who is "full of grace and truth" (John 1:14)—which simply confirms what the Old Testament reveals about the character and saving work of God.[54] The clearest and most straightforward way of resolving this longstanding problem is provided by the gospel.

Because it is the "gospel of the grace of God" (Acts 20:24, NASB), I cannot turn the gospel into an ideology, a set of abstract truths whose supremacy I must achieve in any way that I can. Since the subject of the gospel is the saving love of God, its chief impact wherever it holds sway will be real and growing love for God and for others (1 John 4:9-11, 14-16a, 20-21). So it is the truth that generates love (1 Pet 1:22)—and it is love that makes me passionate about the truth. Since you can only be saved by believing and loving the truth (2 Thess 2:10-13), I have failed to love you as I should if I you wander from the truth because I allowed distortions or perversions of the gospel to go unchallenged.

The gospel has crucial guidance for us at this point also, for it determines both the when and the how of such challenges. The way I confront those who are promoting serious error must match the content of the truth I am seeking to uphold: grace-less behavior brings no honour to the "God of all grace" (1 Pet 5:10) or the gospel of grace. So while I must be firm, I must also be gentle and kind—and while I should present clear arguments, I must not be an argumentative person (2 Tim 2:23-26). And there are some situations in which it would be wrong for me to argue at all. So the same Paul who was prepared to call down God's curse (Gal 1:8-9) and to condemn people as servants of Satan (2 Cor 11:13-15) was also strongly opposed to allowing some disagreements to foster conflict and division.[55] Why didn't he take this second approach in the other situations? And how can I tell when I should fight and when that would be the worst thing I could do? Again, it is the gospel that provides the key.

When the truth of the gospel is at stake, I must not remain silent—for the sake of the lost world, for the sake of Cod's church, and above all for the honour of the Lord Jesus. But when you and I have differing convictions about other matters, I would need to have a very good reason before starting any fights. Christians of earlier times got this right in a

---

[54] Even if we look no wider than the Psalms, there is more than enough evidence of the union of truth and love in who God is and what he does: see (all in the NASB) Psa 25:10; 40:10-11; 57:3, 10; 61:7; 69:13; 85:10; 86:15; 89:14; 108:4; 115:1; 117:2; 138:2.
[55] Rom 14:1-13; 1 Cor 12:21-26; Phil 1:15-17; 3:15; Col 3:11-15.

widely-used motto: "in essentials, unity; in non-essentials, liberty; in all things, charity." The boundary between essentials and non-essentials won't always be easy to define—and when I am in that situation, instead of charging into battle I should first ask its generous Giver for the wisdom I need (Jas 1:5) and then seek advice from believers who have greater insight than me. Once it becomes clear that the gospel is indeed under threat, I have no alternative but to fight for it.[56] But where there is no such threat, how could fighting bring any benefit to the church or any honour to God?

We have seen that any ministry which gives the word of God its rightful place should be conspicuous for its truth and its love. In the previous section, we considered what it means for our ministries to be truth-full. And while we have given some attention to the twin reality of being grace-full, there are some important elements of this we have not yet noted. Because the New Testament says much more about this than we can do justice to here, I have chosen only three examples, all of them reflecting the ways in which God shows his love for us.

One essential feature of the love for which God is both the source and the model is its compassion and kindness (Eph 4:32–5:2). So he does not have unrealistic expectations about what we can do and he does not lay impossible burdens upon us: "he remembers that we are dust" (Psa 103:14). Instead, he is very patient with me, although I am so slow to learn and so quick to get things wrong. The way God deals with us shows that "love is patient, love is kind" (1 Cor 13:4)—and since that is how he treats me, I have no excuse for not treating those I serve and those I serve with in the same way. Any church leader who isn't kind, who treats the members of the church or of its ministry-team in a harsh or callous manner, should have to explain why his conduct is so out of line with the gospel of grace.

One of the most amazing expressions of God's love for us is the way he deals with our sins: "he does not treat us as our sins deserve or repay us according to our iniquities" (Psa 103:10). As a result, I have an obligation to show the same kind of forbearing and forgiving love to others—including my colleagues in ministry—that God lavishes upon

---

[56] Gal 2:3-5, 11-14; Phil 1:27-28; Jude 3-4.

me. This kind of love "is not easily angered, it keeps no record of wrongs" (1 Cor 13:5). And even if I have a legitimate grievance about the way you have treated me, my non-negotiable obligation is to forgive you just as the Lord has forgiven me (Col 3:13). Grudges and grace simply do not mix!

This brings us to a third crucial mark of this love: one that reflects the fact that God's grace towards us is astonishingly rich and lavish (Eph 1:7-8). Because that is so, one of the most obvious signs that his grace is at work is our generosity (2 Cor 8:1-2; 9:13-14). So a grace-filled ministry will be quick to share with others what we have been given—hence Paul's expectation that church leaders will be hospitable.[57] I benefited enormously from being welcomed fully into the home and family life of the pastor who led the first ministry-team I belonged to—which is one of many reasons his name appears at the front of this book.

True generosity does not draw attention to itself: since its only goal is to love by giving, more often than not its beneficiary will not know where the gift has come from (Matt 6:2-4). One of the best gifts my family ever received was a sum of money that came when we really needed it, sent anonymously from a city where we didn't know anybody! But it is not only money that makes a real difference, so I can still be generous even if I have little or no cash to spare. One gift that always matters—although it is easy to neglect—is giving people time and attention. Another is the words of appreciation and encouragement my coworkers should hear from me. And I will soon find many other needs and opportunities for giving, when I go looking for them in the way that a committed giver does.

When Christian ministry gives priority to the gospel as it should, it will be rooted in God's grace and truth. These twin realities ought to mark all of our words and deeds, because together they form the basis and content of all authentic Christian service.

---

[57] 1 Tim 3:2; Tit 1:8; cf. Rom 16:23; Phm 22; 3 John 8.

Worth pondering ...

Now if we have to be gentle with unbelievers ... what shall we do with those who are already children of God? Are they to find no gentleness in us? We must therefore show that we are from the school of him who treats us with nothing but kindness.[58]

[In] regard of the rich grace we offer, we must beseech and entreat with all gentleness ... The power of Christ's ambassadors is a ministry not a domination ... The gospel being a charter of God's love, we must use a dispensation suitable, invite men to God in a loving sweet way ...[59]

If our zeal is embittered by expressions of anger, invective, or scorn, we may think we are doing service to the cause of truth, when in reality we shall only bring it into discredit. The weapons of our warfare, and which alone are powerful to break down the strong-holds of error, are not carnal, but spiritual ...[60]

[What] gives a ministry its motivations, perseverance, humility, joy, tenderness, passion, and grace is the devotional life of the one doing the ministry. When I daily admit how needy I am, daily meditate on the grace of our Lord Jesus Christ, and daily feed on the restorative wisdom of his Word, I am propelled to share with others the grace that I am daily receiving at the hands of my Savior. There is simply no set of exegetical, homiletical, or leadership skills that can compensate for the absence of this in the life of a pastor.[61]

---

[58] John Calvin, Sermons on Titus (Banner of Truth, 2015 [1561]), 233 [on 3:2].
[59] Thomas Manton, Complete Works (Maranatha, n.d.), 13.293.
[60] John Newton, Works, 6 volumes (Banner of Truth, 1985 [1820]), 1.271.
[61] Paul David Tripp, Dangerous Calling: The Unique Challenges of Pastoral Ministry (IVP, 2012), 35.

Part 2: THE SETTING OF CHRISTIAN MINISTRY

2. Christian ministry is determined by God's work

2.1. God is at work, bringing in his salvation and establishing his kingdom

2.1.1. he does this by his Spirit and with his word

2.1.2. we must do God's work in God's way

We have discovered that we must not begin our investigation of Christian ministry with ourselves, and we come now to another reason why this is so. As we have seen, everything about Christian ministry is determined by its foundations. The same is also true of its location: Christian ministry is what it is because of where it happens. It has a context that governs what it is and how it works. This is the fact that God is working out his eternal purpose—and our service fits within this sovereign, saving, kingdom-building work of God. What gives Christian ministry its shape and character is what surrounds and contains it: where it is located determines what it is. So it is not so much about us and what we are doing as about God and what he is doing. To understand ministry properly, we must begin with the work of God.

His work comes before ours, both in time and importance. We serve him because he has served and saved us. What we do for him rests on and responds to what he has done for us. We love—and serve—because he first loved us (1 John 4:19). His work comes first—and it is also much greater than ours in every way: eternal, where ours is quickly over; universal, where ours is very limited; powerful, where ours has many weaknesses; unfailing, where ours is far from certain. So we must not make too much of our ministries. We need to keep reminding ourselves that "neither the one who plants nor the one who waters is anything", since it is only the work of God that produces lasting fruit (1 Cor 3:7). It should therefore be his work and not ours that fills our horizons and gives us confidence: as we serve, we should be glorying in the Lord and his work.[1] So it is vital that we keep going to the Bible to renew our grasp of the glory and grandeur of what God is doing.

---

[1] Rom 15:17-18; 1 Cor 1:28-31.

God's work is thus both the foundation on which ours rests and also the context in which ours takes place. What we do for him must therefore be shaped and controlled by what he is doing: we must do God's work in God's way. What does this actually mean? How is ministry done in God's way different from ministry that is done in some other way? The Bible points us to two essential answers to this question. One of them is this: serving in God's way will mean distancing ourselves from the ways of the world. We must never forget that whoever "chooses to be a friend of the world becomes an enemy of God" (Jas 4:4). If we are determined to be loyal as servants of Jesus and his gospel, then we cannot be people-pleasers (Gal 1:10; 1 Thess 2:4). This relates first of all to our message: if we are true to the gospel, we will not be telling the world what it wants to hear and is prepared to accept. So we must be ready to be unpopular, for the gospel of grace—about a salvation that has been won for us by the work of Another, and to which we contribute nothing except the sin from which we need to be saved—is deeply offensive to human pride. We must also be prepared to be pitied or derided, for even though the gospel is powerful to save, the world writes it off as weak and foolish (1 Cor 1:18-25).

Distancing ourselves from the world involves our methods as well as our message: we will neither accept its standards nor employ its weapons (2 Cor 10:2-5). What the world counts as wisdom is foolishness in God's sight (1 Cor 3:19)—so what it expects and approves will not govern the way we do things. And the world thinks that leaders should be self-assertive and self-promoting, marked by power and prestige rather than humility and self-giving.[2] But we know better, for we belong to the Lord who went all the way down to the bottom, the King who became a pauper and was shamed and disgraced on a cross.[3]

This first answer to our question is all about what we must not do if we are to serve in God's way. But what should we do instead? How do we do God's work in God's way? The second answer the Bible gives us can be put this way: because God does his work by his Spirit and with his word, our ministries must be dependent on his Spirit and focused on his

---

[2]   Mark 10:42-45; 2 Cor 10:12, 17-18; 11:18-21.
[3]   Mark 15:16-20, 31-32; 2 Cor 8:9; Phil 2:7-8; Heb 12:2; 13:13.

word. As we will see in the next few pages, the Bible makes it clear that we are meant to be people of prayer who rely upon the Holy Spirit, and also people who have God's word as the foundation and focus of our ministries. One of the most important points to make about this is that faithful ministries will have the gospel at their heart, because the gospel is fundamental to the work of God.

To understand Christian ministry rightly and to serve God truly, we need to be clear that what we do for him is a small part of the great and glorious work he is doing. Since he gives us a place in his work, we must do God's work in God's way. We must take care that we do not end up doing his work in ways that meekly accept the world's values and follow the world's agenda. Instead, our ministries ought to be marked above all by the Spirit of God, on whom we depend at every point, and the word of God, which is to be the focus and the basis of all that we do. What we need to do now is to discover what the Bible teaches us about each of these fundamental principles of ministry.

Worth pondering ...

[The] Church cannot possibly spring up or be built up by the decrees and doctrines of men... The doctrines of men set up the churches of men, but Christ's Word builds up the Christian Church... having given teachers to the Church our Lord God founds, builds, maintains and enlarges the Church by his Word and his Word alone.[4]

[We] must have [the] confidence that it is the word of God, in the hands of the Spirit of God, that does the work of God.[5]

[We labour] with the external Word—teaching and admonishing; but God, working inwardly through the Spirit, gives the blessing and the success. He permits not our labour with the outward Word to be in vain. Therefore, God is the true Master, performing inwardly the supreme work, while we aid outwardly, serving him through the ministry... For though God is able to effect everything without the instrumentality of the outward Word, working inwardly by his Spirit, this is by no means his purpose. He uses preachers as fellow-workers, or co-labourers, to accomplish his purpose through the Word when and where he pleases.[6]

The Holy Spirit must do his life-giving, eye-opening, blindness-removing, glory-revealing work. The Spirit and the Word are both essential... The Holy Spirit does not do his work apart from the gospel because his work is to open our eyes to see Christ displayed in the gospel, and until the gospel is preached Christ is not there to see... He does his miraculous heart-opening work to make Christ seen and savored as he is preached in the gospel.[7]

Q. What do you believe concerning the holy catholic Church?
A. That the Son of God, out of the whole human race, from the beginning to the end of the world, gathers, defends, and preserves for Himself, by His Spirit and Word, in the unity of the true faith, a Church chosen to everlasting life ...[8]

---

[4] Heinrich Bullinger in G.W. Bromiley (ed), Zwingli and Bullinger, Library of Christian Classics (Westminster, 1953), 307, 309.
[5] David Jackman in William Philip (ed), The Practical Preacher (Christian Focus, 2002), 31f.
[6] Martin Luther, Sermons (Baker, 1983), 7.134.
[7] John Piper, God is the Gospel: Meditations on God's Love as the Gift of Himself (Crossway, 2005), 89, 91.
[8] The Heidelberg Catechism [1563], Lord's Day 21, Question 54.

2. Christian ministry is determined by God's work

2.1. God is at work, bringing in his salvation and establishing his kingdom

2.1.1. he does this by his Spirit[9]

2.1.2. we must do God's work in God's way, relying on the Holy Spirit[10]

We cannot do whatever we like, however we please, and call it Christian ministry! What we do for God is contained within his work, and therefore has to be aligned with what he is doing. Our goals and our methods—and everything else about our work—should reflect his work. We must do God's work in God's way. One of the most crucial things this means is that we are to rely on the Holy Spirit. That is because of where we are in the work of God. His work has reached its decisive climax, with the sending of his Son and then the sending of his Spirit (Gal 4:4-6).

The Old Testament makes it clear that the promised End-time would be Spirit-time. The prophets saw that when God brings in his great salvation and sets up his indestructible kingdom, he will also pour out his Spirit on his people.[11] This will especially mark the ministry of the Messiah, the Servant of the Lord.[12] The New Testament shows us that with the coming of Jesus these promises have reached their fulfilment. We are now in the era of the Spirit.

So when Jesus began his public ministry, the Spirit of God came and remained on him to mark him out as the promised Messiah.[13] From then on, his ministry was empowered and directed by the Spirit.[14] Then as the risen and exalted Lord, he gave the promised Spirit to mark the arrival of

---

9   Luke 24:46-49; John 16:7-15; Acts 1:2, 4-8; 2:1-4, 32-33; 4:31; 5:32; 9:31; Rom 15:18-19; 1 Cor 12:3-7, 12-13; 2 Cor 3:3-8; Eph 3:4-5; 1 Thess 1:4-6; 2 Thess 2:13; 1 Pet 1:1-2, 12.

10   Zech 4:6; Acts 1:8; Rom 15:18-19; 1 Cor 2:3-5; Eph 6:17-20; 2 Tim 1:6-8, 14; 1 Pet 1:12.

11   Isa 32:14-15; 44:1-5; 59:20-21; Ezek 36:25-28; 37:11-14; 39:25-29; Joel 2:28-32.

12   Isa 11:1-3; 42:1-4; 61:1-2.

13   Matt 3:16-17; Mark 1:9-11; Luke 3:21-22; John 1:32-34.

14   Matt 12:28; Luke 3:21-22; 4:1, 14, 16-19; 10:21; John 3:34; Acts 10:38.

the last days.[15] This gift is for all who believe the gospel and turn to him.[16] It is also in a special way for the twelve apostles, to equip them for their mission as Jesus' witnesses to the world.[17] Because it is a fundamental mark of this new covenant age, the apostles' ministry of the gospel is the "ministry of the Spirit".[18] The Spirit equipped them in a special way, with the result that their message is the word of God and their writings are to be received as Scripture.[19] While this applies only to the apostles, the new covenant ministry of the Spirit has not ceased. What began with the apostles still continues, as the gospel is taken to the peoples and nations of the world. Since we are serving in the last days, the era of the Spirit, whatever we do to spread the gospel or build up the church should be done in dependence on the Holy Spirit.[20]

This is a way of saying that the work we do for God must be done with God. That this is necessary becomes obvious as soon as we realize what we are doing. We are not taking heroic and praiseworthy initiatives for a God who is largely inactive and passive. Nor are we completing something God has left unfinished. Rather, by calling us into his service, God has given us a place in the work he is doing. And we are simply not capable of doing that work! Think about it: all those who belong to the world are dead (Eph 2:1; Col 2:13)—and we cannot give them life. They are blind (2 Cor 4:4)—and we cannot make them see. They are lost (Luke 19:10)—and we cannot bring them home. Our world desperately needs to be saved—and only God can save it. Likewise, only God can build the kingdom of God. So if our ministries are to bring God glory, serve his great purposes, and bear lasting fruit, it is absolutely essential that he works with us and through us. In other words, we are totally dependent on the work of the Holy Spirit. As a result, we should be relying upon him consciously and constantly.

---

[15] Luke 3:16; John 1:33; 15:26; 16:7; 20:21-22; Acts 2:14-17, 32-36.

[16] Acts 2:36-39; 11:15-18; 15:7-11; Gal 3:2-8, 14, 22, 26-29; 4:6-7; Eph 1:13-14.

[17] Matt 10:16-20; Luke 24:46-49; John 20:21-22; Acts 1:4-5, 8; 2:1-4.

[18] 2 Cor 2:12, 17; 3:6-8; 4:2-5.

[19] John 14:26; 15:26-27; 16:12-14; 1 Cor 2:12-13; 14:37; Eph 3:4-5; 1 Thess 2:13; 4:2-3, 8; 2 Pet 3:15-16.

[20] Acts 1:8; 1 Cor 12:4-11; 14:12; Eph 4:3-6; 6:17-20; 2 Tim 1:7-8, 14; 3:1; Heb 1:2; Jas 5:3; 1 Pet 1:12,20; 2 Pet 3:3; 1 John 2:18; Jude 18.

This is important for all who are inclined to hold back from Christian service, either because we feel totally inadequate or because we are afraid. The point is that God does not call us into his service and then leave us to rely on our own resources. Given what we are engaged in, that would quickly drive us to despair, for "who is equal to such a task?" (2 Cor 2:16). When it comes to the work of God, it is never the case that we are "competent in ourselves to claim anything for ourselves" (2 Cor 3:5). Instead, God expects us to rely on his Spirit for all that we need. He will help us to deal with the fear and shame that can easily overwhelm us (2 Tim 1:7-8). He will equip us and enable us to do what we could not do on our own.[21] We are not left to work for God without God—so we must make sure that we do not do so.

But is this likely? Why would anyone who knows that Christian ministry is contained within the work God is doing choose to operate without him? It is in fact dismayingly easy for this to happen. One of the most common reasons for this is our pride, which keeps pushing us to be self-confident and self-reliant. Another reason is our forgetfulness. It is not at all uncommon for us to find that we are doing things for God without him. This is not because we have deliberately chosen to go it alone, but because we have drifted into whatever we are doing without remembering to call upon God. The solution in both cases is the same. First, we must keep reminding ourselves that Christian ministry means participating in God's work—and that since only God can do this work, nothing we do for him will be effective unless he is at work with us and through us. We cannot tell ourselves too often that what will never prove to be in vain is not our work, but "the work of the Lord", not our labour, but our labour "in the Lord" (1 Cor 15:58). The second thing we must do is to build many "Nehemiah moments" into the way we live each day (Neh 2:4-5). That is, we must get into the habit of turning to God throughout the day, and calling upon him to empower us and direct us as we work for him.

When we understand what Christian ministry is, it is obvious that our confidence should not rest in ourselves. Instead, it must rest in the Spirit

---

[21] Luke 24:46-49; Acts 1:4-5,8; 4:29, 31; Rom 15:18-19; 2 Cor 3:3-6; Phil 1:19; 4:13; Col 1:29; 2 Tim 1:14; 1 Pet 1:12.

of God, for only he can achieve God's great purposes. This means that we must become praying people, who rely resolutely on God to do what only he can do as we serve him. We are meant to be dependent in carrying out our ministries.

Worth pondering ...

Our whole work must be carried on under a deep sense of our own insufficiency, and of our entire dependence on Christ. We must go for light, and life, and strength to him who sends us on the work. And when we feel our own faith weak, and our hearts dull, and unsuitable to do great a work as we have to do, we must have recourse to him ...[22]

All through history God has chosen and used nobodies, because their unusual dependence on him made possible the unique display of his grace and power. He chose and used somebodies only when they renounced dependence on their natural abilities and resources.[23]

Our God will not be put in the position of an employer who must depend on others to make his business go. Instead He magnifies His all-sufficiency by doing the work Himself... God is not looking for people to work for Him but people who let Him work mightily in and through them ...[24]

It is admirable to see a man humbly conscious of his own weakness, and yet bravely confident in the Lord's power to work through his infirmity.[25]

---

[22] Richard Baxter, The Reformed Pastor (Banner of Truth, 1974 [1656]), 122.
[23] Oswald Chambers, quoted in Kent & Barbara Hughes, Liberating Ministry from the Success Syndrome (Tyndale, 1988), 134.
[24] John Piper, Brothers, We Are Not Professionals: A Plea to Pastors for Radical Ministry, updated and expanded edition (B&H, 2013), 56.
[25] C.H. Spurgeon in Larry J. Michael, Spurgeon on Leadership: Key Insights for Christian Leaders from the Prince of Preachers (Kregel, 2010), 48.

2. Christian ministry is determined by God's work

2.1. God is at work, bringing in his salvation and establishing his kingdom

 2.1.1. he does this by his Spirit and with his word

 2.1.2. we must do God's work in God's way, practicing responsible our dependence[26]

We have discovered that the work we do for God should be done with God. We are not meant to rely on our own resources in serving him. Instead, we must rely on the Spirit of God to equip us with all that we need. Now we are to see that while our dependence on God must be real, it should also be responsible. This means avoiding two common mistakes Christians have often made.

The first mistake is to be completely passive, expecting God to do his work without us. This is often presented as deeply pious, when believers are exhorted to follow slogans like "let go and let God." If we get out of the way, then God will get the job done so much quicker and better! This overlooks the great mercy of God who chooses to use us as he does his work, conferring on us the dignity of being his co-workers (2 Cor 4:1; 6:1). It also forgets that belonging to the Lord Jesus means that we are his servants—and he entrusts us with work we are to do for him. So to leave it all for God to do is to practice irresponsible dependence. Our reliance on him is not meant to be a substitute for our service of him: we must do the work we should do—and yet we must do it in dependence on him.

The second mistake is that of the activist who ends up doing the work without God. Of course, no one will ever exhort us to do this! It is not what any of us will aim at—but it is all too easy for this to be where we end up. So it is vital that we recognize that the work is God's, not ours. To leave God out of the picture is to practice independent responsibility—

---

[26] Rom 15:20, 23-24; 1 Cor 15:10; Col 1:28–2:3; 4:12-13; 2 Thess 1:11-12.

but our service of him is not meant to be done without him. If we leave him out of what we are doing, we are relying on our own abilities and resources. And we simply do not have what it takes to do what the church and the world need so desperately. There is simply no way that we can do God's work by ourselves. Yes, we must do the work we should do—but it must all be done in dependence on him.

So it is not God's work *or* our work, but God's work *and* our work. The house gets built by God—and also by the builders (Psa 127:1)! A better way of expressing this would be to speak of God's work *in* our work, enabling it and using it—or our work with God's work, done in reliance upon him. Although the Bible does not use this term for it, it gives us many examples of this responsible dependence. We will look at just two of them, one from the Old Testament and one from the New. Once you have understood the point by considering these two examples, you will be able to find many others in the Bible.

Our first example comes from the book of Nehemiah. It concerns what happens when Nehemiah learns that his enemies are planning to attack Jerusalem. How does he respond to this threat? He could have stationed sentries on the walls: a response that means "it's all up to us." He could have called a prayer meeting: a response that means "it's all up to God." What he actually did was both of these things: he made sure that the people called upon God and he also posted guards (Neh 4:9). They did what they could and should do—and they also relied on God to protect them and help them. Thanks to Nehemiah, they practiced responsible dependence.

Our second example is where Paul urges Timothy to reflect on what he has written to him (2 Tim 2:7). The reason he gives him for doing this is that the Lord will give him insight into what Paul is saying. Timothy is not meant to try and work it out on his own—but nor is he to sit around and wait for God to tell him what it means. The two are not alternatives but partners: it is not "you think about it—*or* the Lord will give you insight", but "you think about it, **for** the Lord will give you insight." Insight will come from God as Timothy thinks over what Paul says. He should be looking to God while he is looking at the text.

We are to be responsible in ministry and also reliant upon God; we are to practice responsible dependence, dependent responsibility. While this keeps us from doing our own thing, it also releases us to be bold and adventurous in the work of the gospel. Why not dream big dreams and tackle big challenges for the sake of God's kingdom? If Spain is there, why not plan to evangelize it (Rom 15:20, 24, 28)? Such bold initiatives are not, of course, a substitute for faithfulness in the task at hand (Rom 15:19, 23)—and not everyone has either the gifts or the opportunities for the grand projects. But it should be clear that relying on God does not stifle our vision or hold us back from good ventures. Knowing that God usually chooses to use means in doing his work, and that what we do is one of those means, is a stimulus to responsible activity.

Responsible dependence also encourages us to work hard for God and the gospel. That is because he does not leave us to toil away, with nothing but our own resources to rely on. If we attempt to do so, it does not take long for the limitations of our energies and abilities to become very obvious. But when we rely on God, the power of his Spirit energizes us: in our labours he is powerfully at work (Col 1:29). And since there is no limit to this divine empowerment, we can take on big challenges and tough assignments without panicking.

All that we do for God is meant to be done with God. This is necessary because of what we are like: "apart from me you can do nothing" (John 15:5). We must keep reminding ourselves that we are powerless to accomplish God's purpose or to build God's kingdom. At the same time we need to keep reminding ourselves that God never leaves us in the lurch: "he gives strength to the weary and increases the power of the weak" (Isa 40:29). So we must always depend on the Holy Spirit to empower and direct all that we do in God's service. And since we know that God is faithful and can be trusted to work with us, and also that he is gracious and will be pleased to use what we do for him, there is no reason to hang back or to aim small. When it comes to serving God's gospel and kingdom, why shouldn't we give it a red-hot go?

Worth pondering ...

We need to pray that God will show us how rightly to say and do what we ought to say and do, that he will be pleased to use our feeble words and acts, that he will take whatever is right and good in them and that he will overrule all that is wrong and bad, so that in the power of his Spirit they may be his own mighty Word and act. Thrown back upon prayer, however, we make this prayer not in the desperation of a last resort, but in expectant hope.[27]

[Although] our Heavenly Father does not reject our work in cultivating His soil, and does not allow it to be unfruitful, He nevertheless desires its success to depend on His blessing alone, so that all the praise might remain His. Therefore if we want to gain any benefit from our working, our striving, and our pressing on, we should be aware that we shall make no progress unless He prospers our work, our exertions, and perseverance, so that we may commit ourselves and whatever we do to His grace.[28]

[In] husbandry, God hath promised every good thing to us; therefore, let me sit still: the corn will grow, though I sow not nor till the ground. Would not such a one be thought mad, that should reason thus? Because we know that as God hath appointed every end, so he hath ordained order and means, whereby such things shall be effected. Thus it is in grace. He gives 'the will and the deed,' but he prescribes prayer and other ordinances, as the means attaining to this will .... And therefore he bids us hear, read and meditate, watch, and such like, and depend on God for a blessing in the use of the means ... Do that which is required of you. God will do that [that] belongs to him... God is faithful. Use the means, and depend not on the means; but depend on God in the use of the means ...[29]

I hope you will always feel your responsibility before God; but do not carry the feeling too far. We may feel our responsibility so deeply that we become unable to sustain it; it may cripple our joy, and make slaves of us. Do not take an exaggerated view of what the Lord expects of you. He will not blame you for not doing that which is beyond your mental power or physical strength. You are required to be faithful, but you are not bound to be

---

[27] Geoffrey W. Bromiley, "The Ministry of the Word of God" in Christian D. Kettler & Todd H. Speidell (eds), Incarnational Ministry: The Presence of Christ in Church, Society, and Family: Essays in Honor of Ray S. Anderson (Helmers & Howard, 1990), 79-97 (at 96).

[28] John Calvin, Calvin's New Testament Commentaries (Eerdmans, 1960 [1546]), 9.70f [on 1 Cor 3:7].

[29] Richard Sibbes, Works (Banner of Truth, 1977 [1639]), 5.18, 19 [on Phil 2:13].

successful. You are to teach, but you cannot compel people to learn. You are to make things plain, but you cannot give carnal men an understanding of spiritual things. We are not the Father, nor the Saviour, nor the Comforter of the Church.[30]

---

[30] Charles H. Spurgeon, An All-Round Ministry (Banner of Truth, 1960 [1900]), 214.

2. Christian ministry is determined by God's work

2.1. God is at work, bringing in his salvation and establishing his kingdom

2.1.1. he does this with his word, which is powerful and accomplishes his purpose[31]

2.1.2. we must do God's work in God's way, so his word must be the focus and the foundation of our ministries[32]

The word of God is meant to be at the heart of all Christian service. That is because God does his work by and with his word. And his word is effective: it always accomplishes his purpose (Isa 55:10-11). What is this word that is the powerful agent of God's saving purpose? It is, of course, the gospel (Rom 1:16). It is by the gospel that God is doing his saving work in the world, establishing his kingdom and gathering his church into eternal glory.[33] The gospel is not just words, as a merely human message is. It is alive and active; it grows and spreads; it bears fruit; it comes with power.[34] It brings salvation and eternal life to those who believe.[35] It is the means by which God gives us new birth (Jas 1:18; 1 Pet 1:23-25). It goes on doing God's work in the lives of his people (1 Thess 2:13), producing the fruit of godliness in us (Tit 1:1; 2 Pet 1:4). It is the means by which God builds his people up, brings us to our heavenly inheritance (Acts 20:32) and gives us a share in the glory of Christ (2 Thess 2:14). And since we must do God's work in God's way, the gospel should be at the heart and the root of our ministries.

---

31 Isa 55:10-11; Acts 6:7; 12:24; 19:20; 20:32; Rom 1:16; 16:25; Col 1:5-6; 1 Thess 2:13; 2 Thess 2:13-14; Heb 4:12; Jas 1:18, 21; 1 Pet 1:23-25.

32 Matt 28:19-20; Acts 2:42; 5:42; 6:4; 11:19-21; 15:35; 18:5, 11; 28:30-31; 1 Cor 1:17-25; 4:17; 15:1-2; Eph 1:13; 4:20-21; Col 1:28; 3:16; 1 Thess 2:8-9, 13; 1 Tim 4:13-16; 2 Tim 2:2, 15, 24-25; 4:2; Tit 1:9; 2:1, 15; Heb 13:7; 1 Pet 1:22-25.

33 Matt 24:14; Acts 13:44-49; 18:9-11; Rom 15:15-19; 16:25-26; 1 Cor 1:17-25; 15:1-2; 2 Cor 4:1-6; Col 1:5-6; 1 Thess 2:13; 2 Thess 2:13-14.

34 Mark 4:14, 20; Acts 6:7; 12:24; 19:20; 1 Cor 2:4-5; 2 Cor 4:4-7; Col 1:6; 1 Thess 1:4-5; 2 Thess 3:1; Heb 4:12.

35 Acts 13:26, 46; 16:30-32; Rom 1:16; 1 Cor 15:1-2; Eph 1:13; Jas 1:21.

It is important not to misunderstand this point. We are not saying that Christian ministry is limited to the gospel but that it is centred on the gospel and based on the gospel. Here it is helpful to recognize that the expression "the word of God" can be used in two ways. Most often, the New Testament uses it to refer to the gospel.[36] But it can also be used of the Bible, which is God speaking to us.[37] The Bible's human words are given by the Spirit of God (2 Tim 3:16). This is true not only of the writings of the prophets (2 Pet 1:21), but also of the writings of the apostles. These too are Scripture (2 Pet 3:16), the word of the Lord (1 Cor 14:37), Spirit-given words that impart Spirit-given understanding of God and his work (1 Cor 2:12-13).

What is the relation between these two forms of "the word of God": that is, how is the gospel related to the Bible? God's gospel word is the centre and focus of his scriptural word. As Jesus is the centre and meaning of the gospel, so the gospel is the centre and meaning of the Bible. It is not only the New Testament but also the Old Testament that bears witness to Jesus and the gospel.[38] What the New Testament does is to expound the gospel and also to explore its implications for Christian devotion and discipleship, Christian life and ministry. The apostles unpack the gospel, taking it deeper in relation to needs and problems that have emerged in their churches. They also apply the gospel, pushing it wider to show how it should be lived out across a wide range of issues and problems.

So the Bible is to be our focus and foundation—but because the gospel is the centre of the Scriptures, that makes the gospel the heart and the root of our lives and ministries. And because this is how God does his work, our overriding aim will be to make the gospel known, to get it into the public domain and to lodge it in people's minds and lives. We will want it to spread rapidly (2 Thess 3:1), to keep on doing its work in believers' lives (1 Thess 2:13), and to hold a central place in our life

---

[36] Luke 5:1; 8:11, 21; 11:28; Acts 4:31; 6:2, 7; 8:14, 25; 11:1; 12:24; 13:15, 44, 46, 48-49; 15:35-36; 16:32; 17:13; 18:11; 19:10, 20; 1 Cor 14:36; 2 Cor 2:17; 4:2; Phil 1:14; Col 1:25; 1 Thess 2:13; 2 Tim 2:9; Tit 2:5; Heb 4:12; 5:12; 6:5; 13:7; 1 Pet 1:23-25; Rev 1:2, 9; 6:9; 20:4.

[37] Matt 15:6; 22:29, 31-32, 43; John 10:35; Acts 1:16; 4:25-26; 28:25; Rom 9:6; Heb 1:1, 5-13; 3:7-11; 4:7; 5:5-6; 8:8-12; 10:15-17, 30; 13:5.

[38] Luke 24:25-27, 44-47; John 5:39, 46; Acts 3:18, 21; 10:43; 13:27; 28:23; Rom 1:1-4; 3:21; 1 Cor 15:1-4; 2 Tim 3:15; 1 Pet 1:10-12.

together (Col 3:16). We must keep bringing God's word to people—and we must keep bringing people to God's word.

But we must not only bring others to God's word; we must keep coming to it ourselves. God's effective word is also his instructive word: it teaches us his will—not only for our lives but also for our ministries. So the Bible is our ministry manual: it gives us the content of our message and it also teaches us the character of our ministry—and a ministry shaped and governed by God's word is one in which the gospel has the decisive role. To understand what Christian ministry is meant to be, we must begin with the gospel.

We began our exploration of Christian ministry by insisting that it can only be understood if we start with Jesus the Servant-Lord. So why are we now saying that we should begin with the gospel? This does not represent a change of mind; it is just a different way of making the same point. That is because the gospel is the word of Christ that declares the worth of Christ (who he is) and the work of Christ (what he has done for us). To begin with the gospel is thus to ground our understanding and practice of ministry on who Jesus is, and on what he has done to serve and save us. This will lead to ministries that are rooted in, centred on, and expressive of the grace of God. It will produce servants who are prepared to keep growing down in humility, to be last and least and lowest, to suffer loss for Jesus and the gospel.[39] It will have us doing God's work in God's way.

We need to be vigilant here: if God's word does not determine the way we serve, then the world around us will. That is because we are always tempted to take the path of least resistance, to do what is most popular. And the resulting ministry will often appear to be successful, because there is nothing the world likes better than having its own priorities and fashions endorsed and followed. But we will only produce fruit that lasts, fruit that pleases God, if we are ruled not by the world but by the word.

---

[39] Matt 23:8-12; Mark 8:35; 10:28-31; John 13:13-16; 15:18-20; Acts 5:41; 20:22- 24; 1 Cor 4:9-13; 10:31-33; 2 Cor 6:3-10; 11:23-29; Phil 1:27–2:4; 2:20- 22, 29-30; 2 Thess 1:3-5; 2 Tim 1:8; 2:8-10; 3:10-13; 4:5; Heb 10:32-36; 11:35–12:3; 13:11-13; 1 Pet 4:12-19; Rev 2:3, 9-10, 13.

The gospel must be our focus and foundation: all authentic Christian ministry will have the word of God at its heart and at its root. Without this powerful word, we would have no way of growing the church or winning the world. Without his word to teach us, we would have no way of knowing how God wants us to serve him in the church and the world. Christian ministry is meant to be shaped and governed by God's effective, instructive word.

Worth pondering ...

The words of God in Scripture are the building blocks of the church. As pastors and church leaders, then, our first priority is to make sure that the Gospel enjoys functional centrality in the church. That is, we must make sure that the Gospel governs the way the church functions... God's Word, encapsulated in the Gospel, builds the church.[40]

Programs don't save anyone. Events don't save anyone. Strategies don't save anyone. Décor doesn't save anyone. Atmosphere doesn't save anyone. Preachers don't save anyone. God saves people. And he does it through the message of the gospel... Knowing and trusting that the gospel is God's power for salvation means that your trust in the gospel filters down into how you do your ministry. It means making sure that the gospel is the foundation, the shape, the method, the means, the content, and the very centre of your ministry and leadership. The gospel is God's power to save. Trust it in everything you do.[41]

Let us persevere with our task and leave the success to the Lord ... let us give the word; and God will give the Spirit; let us plant and water; and God in due time will give the increase... Such is the power of the word of God that to effect nothing and to profit no-one is impossible.[42]

The ministry of the word must have pride of place in the church of Jesus Christ. Other ministries in the church matter—a lot. But the ministry of the word must be primary precisely because the word of God gives life and sustains life... The emphasis in Scripture suggests that we must make it the centerpiece of church growth. God has always created his people by his word, and he always will...[43]

The gospel, for Paul, is not just a door that you walk through at the start of the Christian life, but a rock that you stand on for the rest of your days... Those of us who are called to serve as leaders, teachers, and preachers among God's people must therefore never be embarrassed of ... evangelizing the church, reminding God's people of the gospel that they depend upon every day... The same applies to the work of a Bible study leader or a youth pastor or a father or a mother ...[44]

---

[40] Mark Dever & Paul Alexander, The Deliberate Church: Building Your Ministry on the Gospel (Crossway, 2005), 21-22.

[41] Craig Hamilton, Wisdom in Leadership (Matthias Media, 2015), 41.

[42] John Jewel, Works, (Cambridge: CUP, 1847 [ca.1551]), 2.954f (updated).

[43] Jason Meyer, Preaching: A Biblical Theology (Crossway, 2013), 305 (his italics).

[44] David I. Starling, UnCorinthian Leadership: Thematic Reflections on 1 Corinthians (Cascade, 2014), 66.

2. Christian ministry is determined by God's work

2.1. God is at work, bringing in his salvation and establishing his kingdom

2.1.1. he does this with his word, which is powerful and accomplishes his purpose

2.1.2. we must do God's work in God's way, so his word must be the focus and the foundation of our ministries

We must keep holding it fast:[45] we must never alter it,[46] and we must never abandon it.[47] We must keep making it known, both widely throughout the world,[48] and also deeply in the church.[49]

The word of God is absolutely central in the work of God. He does his saving, kingdom-building work by and with his word. This means that we must make his word the focus in all the work we do for him: we must keep bringing God's word to people and bringing people to God's word. And his word must also be the basis on which our own lives and ministries are built.

This must be true of the way we live as Christians: we are to keep on hearing and heeding, reading and responding to the word of God. It must shape all that we are and all that we do. So it is vital that we feed upon his word continually, letting it do its work in us. It must take root in our hearts, so that it bears fruit in our lives.[50] This means that we must keep on exploring it, pondering it, and taking it in.[51] We must also keep on living it out: we are meant to live in obedience to God's word.[52] This needs to be said because of one of the dangers we face in ministry: that I can

---

45 Phil 2:16; 1 Tim 3:9; 6:20; 2 Tim 1:13-14; Tit 1:9; 1 John 2:24; Rev 3:3.
46 2 Cor 4:2; Gal 1:6-9; Rev 22:18-19.
47 John 8:31-32; Col 1:23; 2:6-7; 2 Thess 2:15; 1 John 2:24; 2 John 9; Rev 2:24-25.
48 Psa 9:7-11; 96:3-10; 105:1; Isa 12:4-5; Matt 24:14; 28:19-20; Luke 24:45-47; Acts 1:8; 8:4; 13:46-47; Rom 15:18-24.
49 Acts 11:25-26; 18:9-11; 19:8-10; 20:20, 27, 31; Col 1:25-28; 2 Pet 1:12-15; 3:1-2.
50 Deut 6:5-6; 11:18; 30:14; Psa 1:2-3; 37:30-31; 40:8; 119:11; Luke 8:11, 15; Col 1:6-7.
51 Josh 1:8; Psa 1:1-2; 119:15, 97, 99, 148; Acts 17:11; 2 Tim 2:7-8; Rev 3:3.
52 Psa 119:4, 17, 57, 101; Rom 6:17; 15:18-19; Gal 5:7; Jas 1:22; 1 Pet 1:22-25.

end up viewing God's word as meant for "them" and not for me. I have to make sure that whatever I preach or teach to others I have first applied to myself, so that I really do take it in and live it out. Remember how Paul tells Timothy that the Scriptures are "useful for teaching, rebuking, correcting and training in righteousness" (2 Tim 3:16). He says this not primarily to show Timothy how he should use the Scriptures in his ministry to others, but because this is how he wants Timothy to use the Scriptures on himself! Timothy is the "servant of God" who is to be "thoroughly equipped for every good work" by the Scriptures (2 Tim 3:17).

God's word must be just as central in our ministries as it is in our lives. We have nothing to offer the church or the world but God's gospel word, the word of Christ that declares the worth of Christ and the work of Christ. But this is just what both the church and the world need—and need desperately—and need constantly. So we must never tire of holding out God's word—and we must never start offering something else instead. We must never replace or revise the gospel. We must not give up on the gospel, and replace it with some alternative. Because there is no salvation without the gospel, putting anything else in its place will certainly bring God's judgment.[53] Besides, how could we think that anything we concoct would be capable of winning the world for Christ or perfecting the church in Christ? Nor must we tamper with the gospel. We have no right to do so, because it is not ours. And we have no reason to do so, because it powerfully accomplishes God's saving purpose. It does not need to be amended or improved to make it more marketable. It does not need to be propped up on crutches borrowed from the world. It does need to be declared publicly and privately, explained and applied, commended and defended.

We should be working as hard as we can to see that God's gospel spreads wider and wider throughout the world and penetrates deeper and deeper into the lives of his people. If this deep work is to happen, one of the most important tasks we must work at is the ministry of reminding.[54] All too easily we get things out of focus; all too often we forget what matters most. Most of the time, our greatest need is not to learn

---

[53] 2 Cor 11:3-5, 13-15; Gal 1:8-9; Jude 3-4.
[54] 1 Cor 15:1-2; Phil 3:1; 2 Tim 2:14; 2 Pet 1:12-15; 3:1-2; Jude 5.

THE SETTING OF CHRISTIAN MINISTRY

something new but to recall what we know already: we need to be reminded of Jesus and the gospel, so that we prove faithful to him in every part of our lives.

When it comes to making God's word known, we must keep on keeping on. Nothing else will produce lasting fruit for his kingdom. And nothing else will bring God the glory he must have. But what if I do not have a "ministry of the word"? What if my ministry is serving rather than teaching or speaking God's words (Rom 12:7; 1 Pet 4:11)? Three points are worth making here. First, while I may not get to "preach the word" (2 Tim 4:2), I will still speak lots of words! I must watch what I say, wanting all of my words to be full of grace and truth.[55] And as often as I can, I will want to bear witness to Jesus and the gospel. Secondly, we are all meant to live in a way that is worthy of the gospel (Phil 1:27), that lines up with the gospel and makes it attractive (Tit 2:1-10). If I do this, my life will be out of step with the world—and that will create openings to explain my gospel priorities and values (1 Pet 3:15). Thirdly, even if I am not a preacher, how could I be content to have no "ministry of the word"? Everybody needs to know God's word and to live by it. So I should be finding or creating regular opportunities to open the Bible with others: in my family; leading a Bible study in my home; reading the Bible each week with one or two others; getting involved in my church's children's program—there is plenty that could and should be done in this essential area of Christian work.

Knowing that God does his saving, kingdom-building work by means of the gospel is important for all those who are very conscious of their weaknesses and failings. What am I to tell myself when I feel completely inadequate to be a messenger of God's life-giving word? Here too I must begin with the gospel. I must preach it to myself again, as I need to do regularly if my ministry is to stay on course. Doing so will remind me that God is not in the business of giving prizes to the outstanding but of showing mercy to the wretched. So ministry is not a reward for the deserving but a gift to the unworthy—and this means that I am not disqualified even though I am as ordinary and breakable as a clay jug (2 Cor 4:7). I also need to remember that the world regards the gospel's

---

55   Matt 12:36-37; Eph 4:15, 29; 5:4; Col 4:6; Jas 3:2-12; 4:11.

message about a crucified Lord and Saviour as weak and foolish—although in fact it embodies God's power and wisdom.[56] And the work of God is just as counter-cultural as the word of God: he usually does his work through people who are not impressive by the standards of the world.[57] There is in fact no one who is too weak or too lowly to be used by God.

Whatever my ministry, I will want to make as much as possible of the word of God. I must keep holding it fast: believing it and obeying it, building my life and ministry on it. And I must keep holding it out, making it known as widely and deeply as I can.

---

[56] Rom 1:16; 1 Cor 1:18, 22-25.

[57] 1 Cor 1:26-29; 4:9-13; 2 Cor 4:7-12; 6:3-10; 10:10; 11:23-29; 12:9-11; Gal 4:13-14; Eph 3:13.

Worth pondering ...

There is only one pure gospel, as also there is only one Lord Jesus Christ on whom it is founded. It is not for us to create the gospel anew; indeed, if we seek to add anything to the pure seed which we have received from our Lord Jesus Christ, we are destroying what God has established... How dreadful it is that the gospel, the foundation of our salvation, and the key that opens the gates of paradise, should be perverted! It is our only treasure... we must cling with strong affection to the gospel, and not allow anyone to corrupt it in any way.[58]

[At] the core of Christian leadership—as an extension of Christian life and faithfulness—is your constant commitment to trust the Bible. Will God's word shape your life and your leadership? ... The degree to which your leadership is built on, shaped by, conforms to, and is accountable to God's word is the degree to which your leadership will be Christ-honouring and kingdom-building ...[59]

[He] who doth not, or can not, or will not feed the flock is no pastor ... A man is a pastor unto them whom he feeds by pastoral teaching ... and he that doth not so feed is no pastor... how great a necessity there is incumbent on all pastors of churches to give themselves unto the word and prayer, to labour in the word and doctrine, to be continually intent on this work, to engage all the faculties of their souls, to stir up all their graces and gifts, unto constant exercise in the discharge of their duty ...[60]

The faithful evangelist, pastor and teacher must become an unceasing and unfailing servant and minister of the God-given word, giving himself to its ministry and to accompanying prayer as his primary task, always quoting it as his authority, and proving as he does so that the living God is still active by His Spirit to use His word to do His saving work in the hearts and lives of men and women.[61]

---

[58] John Calvin, Sermons on Galatians (Banner of Truth, 1997 [1563]), 35, 44.
[59] Craig Hamilton, Wisdom in Leadership (Matthias Media, 2015), 32.
[60] John Owen, Works (Banner of Truth, 1968 [1689]), 16.75, 77.
[61] Alan Stibbs in Andrew Atherstone (ed), Such a Great Salvation: The Collected Essays of Alan Stibbs (Mentor, 2008), 209.

2. Christian ministry is determined by God's work

> 2.2. God includes us in the work he is doing
>
> > 2.2.1. God does not need anything we can do for him[62]
> >
> > 2.2.2. yet he gives us a place in his work, conferring on us the great dignity of being his co-workers[63]
> >
> > 2.2.3. so all ministry is a privilege, a gift from a gracious God[64]

At the foundation of all Christian ministry lies God and his grace. We have already noted some of the chief ways in which this is true. However, one that we have only touched on briefly is so important that it needs to be given special attention. This is the fact that Christian ministry is itself a gift. We are not in ministry because God needs us (Acts 17:25), so we are not doing him a favour by serving him. In fact, it is the other way around: he has shown us immense favour by calling us into his service. The God of the Bible does not need us to get his work done. He made the entire cosmos without any help from us – and he is perfectly able to save the world without our input! But he chooses not to do so. Out of his great kindness he makes room for us and gives us a place in his work. All ministry stems from God's mercy (2 Cor 4:1).

This becomes clear when we look at any of the chief elements in Christian ministry. Consider the crucial task of evangelism. According to the Bible, it is the Lord himself who takes the lead in this absolutely essential work. He is the one who seeks and saves the lost (Luke 19:10). He calls and finds and gathers his sheep.[65] He speaks in the gospel, calling people to himself.[66] Salvation belongs to our God (Rev 7:10; 19:1)

---

[62] 1 Chron 29:10-16; Psa 50:9-13; Acts 17:25.
[63] Acts 14:27; 15:4, 12; 21:19; Rom 15:18; 1 Cor 3:5-9; 12:5-6; 15:58; 16:10; 2 Cor 2:14; 5:18–6:1; Phil 2:30; 1 Thess 3:2; 2 Tim 4:17; Tit 1:3.
[64] Rom 1:5; 15:15-16; 2 Cor 4:1; Eph 3:7-8; Col 4:17.
[65] Ezek 34:11-12, 16; Luke 15:1-6; John 10:16.
[66] Rom 15:18-19; 2 Cor 5:20; 2 Thess 2:13-14; 1 Pet 2:9.

and he is the only Saviour[67]—not only because he has worked it for us in his Son, but also because he is the one who brings us in and gives us a place in that great salvation.[68] So whatever we do in our evangelism, we are no more than his junior partners, privileged to be working with him. The same is true of the vital work of pastoring, caring for God's flock. The true pastor is the Lord himself, for the Bible tells us that he is the chief shepherd, the great shepherd of the sheep.[69] The sheep belong to him and not to us, and he looks after them.[70] Yet he does not exclude us from this work: he makes room for other shepherds (which is what "pastor" means) to join in caring for his flock.[71] He is also the one who builds his church.[72] Again, he gives us a role in this great work.[73] So our shepherding and church-building—along with all the other aspects of our ministries—is not only done for him, it is also done with him. He gives us the great privilege of being his co-workers.[74]

It is important not to take this the wrong way. We must never give the impression that this is a partnership between equals! Fundamentally, this is his work: there is a sense in which all of it is done by him—and yet for the most part, he does it not without us but with us and through us.[75] But he does not need to work like this. He chooses to do so because he is "the God of all grace" (1 Pet 5:10). Our ministries are an expression of his kindness to us—a gift he did not have to give, not a tool he had to use. And it is vital that we hold fast to this fact, for we will only cause problems if we don't do so. Here is an example of how this can happen: keen to make sure that we all pull our weight in God's work, Christians have sometimes used the slogan, "he has no hands but our hands and no feet but our feet." Despite the good intentions involved, this can easily give people the wrong

---

[67] Deut 32:15; 1 Chron 16:35; ; Psa 65:5; 68:19-20; 79:9; 85:4; Isa 17:10; 43:3, 11; 45:21; 60:16; 62:11; Luke 2:11; John 4:42; Acts 4:12; 13:23; 1 Tim 1:1; 2:3; Tit 1:3-4; 2:10, 13; 3:4, 6; 1 John 4:14; Jude 25.
[68] Acts 2:47; 1 Cor 6:11; Eph 2:4-9; Phil 2:12-13; Col 1:12-14; 2:13; Tit 3:4-7.
[69] John 10:11, 14; Heb 13:20; 1 Pet 2:25; 5:4.
[70] John 10:3-4, 14, 25-28.
[71] Acts 20:28; Eph 4:11; 1 Pet 5:2-4.
[72] Matt 16:18; Eph 2:19-22; 4:16; 1 Pet 2:5.
[73] 1 Cor 3:10-15; 8:1; 14:12, 26; 2 Cor 10:8; 13:10; Eph 4:12, 16; 1 Thess 5:11.
[74] 1 Cor 3:9, NASB; 2 Cor 6:1; 1 Thess 3:2, NASB.
[75] Acts 14:27; 15:4, 12; 21:19; Rom 15:18; 1 Cor 3:5; 2 Cor 2:14; 2 Tim 4:17; Tit 1:3.

impression. It implies that we are much more important than we really are, and thus puts us under a pressure we are not meant to carry. If the slogan is right, any mistake or failure on my part threatens to derail the work of God—and if I give my hands and feet a rest just for a little while, his work will come to a halt! Laying such a burden on us is bad enough, but even worse is the way it diminishes God. By making me essential, it suggests that he is limited and dependent—and thus very far removed from the sovereign Redeemer and Ruler we meet in the Bible.

So there is no gaping hole in the work of God, needing to be filled by what we do. In this in-between time, between Easter and the End, he has not retreated or retired. He is still powerfully at work, advancing his great purpose for the world.[76] And by giving us our ministries he has included us in what he is doing—and has thus given us great significance. Although we are only servants, we really matter, not because we are needed for his work but because he has chosen to include us in it. Yet even at its best, our work is always eclipsed by the much greater work in which it plays a part. So we should not make too much of our ministries, as though they—and therefore we—were something special. Instead, we should often be saying to the Lord, "All that we have accomplished you have done for us" (Isa 26:12). And we should often be saying to each other, "The Lord has done this, and it is marvellous in our eyes" (Psa 118:23). There is no room for pride here. It is God's works and not ours that are great and glorious. It is what he does that should arouse our wonder and delight.[77]

In view of all this, we should serve gratefully, recognizing that it is a great privilege to participate in God's work. We should also serve confidently, because God's work cannot fail. And we should serve humbly, because all that we do is only a very small part of something great—and because our contribution is always far from perfect. Above all, we should serve in a way that aims at the glory of God. In Christian ministry too, everything is "from him and through him and for him". The only right response to this is, "To him be the glory forever!" (Rom 11:36).

---

[76] John 5:17; 1 Cor 1:8-9; 3:5-7; 6:11; 10:13; 11:32; 12:3, 12-13, 28; 15:9-10; Gal 2:8; Eph 3:20; Phil 1:6; 2:12-13; 1 Thess 1:4-5; 2:13; 3:12-13; 4:9; 5:23-24; 1 Pet 1:1-2.

[77] Psa 66:2, 5; 72:18; 86:10; 92:5; 96:3; 107:8, 15, 21, 31; 111:2-3; 136:4; 145:4-6.

Worth pondering...

[When] it pleases God to call someone to be responsible for preaching the gospel, he is granting him a singular mercy. God does this, not only so that we who have this role and position should walk in his fear, attributing nothing to ourselves, but also so that each of us may be a living testimony to the love that God bears to his church.[78]

Just as we are to be constantly reminding our hearers that the world does not revolve around them, so we must be doubly diligent to remind ourselves that ministry is not all about us. Everything is about Him. We are His. The Church is His. The ministry is His. He allows us the unspeakable honor of laboring with Him—though we are nothing in ourselves.[79]

It is a wonder of condescendence, that the Lord will make use of men in promoting [people's salvation]. To be workers together with God in so great a business, is no small honour. The great value of men's souls, the greatness of the misery they are delivered from, and of the happiness they are advanced to, with the manifold glory of God shining in all, makes the work of saving men great and excellent. Preaching the gospel, and suffering for it, are services that angels are not employed in.[80]

God has always used His ministers for the gathering or erecting of a Church to Himself, and for the governing and preservation of the same; and still He does, and always will, use them so long as the Church remains on earth... True it is that God can, by His power, without any means, take unto Himself a Church from among men; but He had rather deal with men by the ministry of men... we must take heed that we do not attribute too much to the ministers and ministry ... Therefore let us believe that God does teach us by His Word, outwardly through His ministers, and does inwardly move and persuade the hearers of His elect unto belief by His Holy Spirit; and that therefore we ought to render all the glory of this whole benefit unto God.[81]

---

[78] John Calvin, Sermons on Galatians (Banner of Truth, 1997 [1563]), 83.
[79] Reid Ferguson, The Little Book of Things You Should Know About Ministry (Christian Focus, 2002), 109f.
[80] Robert Traill, Works (Banner of Truth, 1975 [1682]), 1.244.
[81] The Second Helvetic Confession [1566], XVIII.1, 2.

2. Christian ministry is determined by God's work

2.3. Our work is framed by God's work

2.3.1. we serve between the comings of Jesus: his past completed work and his future completing work[82]

Christian ministry is not fundamentally about us but about God and his work—and his great kindness in giving us a place in it. Its content and character should therefore be governed by the will and ways of God. At every point, it is meant to be shaped by what God is doing and how he is doing it. This great work of God forms the context in which we carry out our ministries: our work is framed by his work.

This work of God has a particular shape. We can think of it as like a bridge held up by two great pylons, one at each end. One pylon is Easter: this is the work the Lord Jesus completed in his death and resurrection-exaltation. The other pylon is the End: this is the work Jesus will complete at his coming in glory. Our ministries fit on the bridge, bounded by what Jesus has already done for us at Easter and what he is going to do with us at the End. This does not mean that God's work is confined to the pylons, so that the bridge itself is formed by what we do. The pylons represent what he does without us; the bridge is where he brings our work in alongside his. So at one end, we have the work of Jesus the redeeming and risen Lord; at the other end, the work of Jesus the returning Lord—and in the middle, the work of Jesus the reigning Lord. This is what he does from heaven, in contrast to what he did on earth (Acts 1:1-2). While he is there, seated at the Father's right hand,[83] he is not idle: he is powerfully at work in his people and in the world.[84] This is where our ministries fit, as he works with us and through us.

The nature of Christian ministry is determined by its location between Easter and the End. This gives it an "in-between" character, since

---

[82] 1 Tim 2:5-7; 6:11-15; 2 Tim 1:8-14; 4:1-2, 8; Heb 9:24-28; 1 Pet 1:3-7, 13, 18-21; 1 John 2:28–3:2; 4:9-10, 13-14.

[83] Acts 2:33-34; 5:31; Rom 8:34; Eph 1:20; Col 3:1; Heb 1:3; 8:1; 10:12; 12:2; 1 Pet 3:22.

[84] Acts 2:47; 11:21; 16:14; 18:9; 2 Cor 2:12; 1 Thess 3:12; 2 Thess 2:16-17; 3:3, 5, 16; 2 Tim 2:7; 3:11; 4:17-18; 2 Pet 1:1, 3-4; Rev 2:1, 16, 22; 3:3, 7-8, 19-20.

it is shaped by the "already" of Easter and also by the "not yet" of the End. The first gives us our foundation: it is what we look back to and build on. The second forms our destination: it is what we must still wait for and work for. Both of these anchor-points are meant to have a big impact on the way we serve.

The past work of the Lord Jesus gives us our foundation, the basis on which all of our service rests. This is where we began, when we learned that Christian ministry is grounded on Jesus the Servant-Lord and also on God's grace and truth. What he did for us when he came into the world as its Saviour is the heart of our message and the root of our ministries.[85] All that we say and all that we do as his servants arises above all out of Jesus' death and resurrection-exaltation. By his death, he bought us and claims us; because he died for us, we live for him; because he has served and saved us, we now serve him.[86] Because he was raised to be Lord of all, we belong to him; because he rules, we are his servants; because he has been given all authority in heaven and on earth, we live in obedience to him.[87] By his death and resurrection he has won the decisive victory over sin and death and Satan.[88] This is D-day, the victory that guarantees his complete and final triumph at the End. The salvation we are waiting for (we will be saved) is when he implements fully the salvation he has already established and secured (we have been saved).[89]

Christian ministry thus rests on an unshakeable foundation. What we are doing relies on and responds to what he has done. As a result, we have every reason to set about our work eagerly and joyfully, privileged to have a place in something so great and glorious.

The future work of the Lord Jesus gives us our destination, the goal to which all of our service is heading. We are working towards the great

---

[85] Matt 1:21; Luke 2:11; John 3:17; 4:42; 1 Tim 1:15; 2 Tim 1:10; 1 John 4:14.
[86] Mark 10:43-45; Acts 20:28; 1 Cor 6:19-20; 7:22-23; 2 Cor 5:15; Tit 2:14; Rev 5:9-10.
[87] Matt 28:18-20; Luke 6:46; Rom 14:7-9; 16:18; 1 Cor 12:5; Heb 5:9; 1 Pet 1:2.
[88] Rom 5:17-21; 6:9-13; 1 Cor 15:20-26, 57; Col 2:15; 2 Tim 1:10; Heb 2:14-15; 9:12-15, 26-28; 10:12-14; 1 John 1:7; 2:2; 3:5, 8; 4:10; Rev 3:21; 5:5.
[89] Rom 5:9-10; 8:15-25; Eph 1:3-14; 2:4-9; 1 Thess 1:4-5, 9-10; 5:8-10, 23; 2 Tim 1:9-10; 2:10; 4:18; Tit 2:11-14; 3:4-7; Heb 9:26-28; 10:12-14; 1 Pet 1:3-5.

Day that is coming,[90] when Jesus returns to our world as Saviour and as Judge.[91] How should this coming climax shape our ministries? Because the final triumph of Jesus is secure and certain, we ought to serve gladly and confidently, knowing that our labour is not in vain (1 Cor 15:57-58). This should also make us tenacious and persevering, not easily daunted or likely to give up (2 Cor 4:14-18). As we look forward to this coming glory, we also learn to live by the logic of the kingdom. This is captured well in the motto of Jim Elliott, the missionary who was martyred in Ecuador in 1956: "He is no fool who gives what he cannot keep to gain what he cannot lose." The fact that we are destined to see and share the glory of the Lord Jesus, to enter into God's heavenly kingdom and take possession of our heavenly inheritance, should make us ready to endure suffering and make sacrifices for his sake.[92] We also know that the Lord Jesus is coming to judge us and reward us.[93] This gives us a strong incentive to serve with integrity, to be rigorous in our self-discipline and relentless in the fight against our own sinfulness. It also counteracts the desire we often have to be praised and esteemed by those we serve, which so easily makes us unfaithful by turning us into people-pleasers. Looking to the coming Day reminds us that the verdict that counts is not now but then, not ours but his. It also teaches us the need for patience and persistence, because ministry is for the long haul: our work is not done until the End. And some of the most important aspects of what we are doing take time and cannot be rushed, because we are building for eternity, aiming for fruit that lasts.[94]

Christian ministry fits within the work God is doing. Its location between Easter and the End gives it its special character, based on an

---

90 Matt 7:22; 10:15; 11:22, 24; 12:36; 24:36, 42, 50; 25:13; Acts 17:31; Rom 2:5, 16; 13:12; 1 Cor 1:8; 3:13; 5:5; 2 Cor 1:14; Eph 4:30; Phil 1:6, 10; 2:16; 1 Thess 5:2, 4, 5, 8; 2 Thess 1:10; 2:2, 3; 2 Tim 1:12, 18; 4:8; Heb 10:25; 1 Pet 2:12; 2 Pet 2:9; 3:7, 10, 12; 1 John 4:17; Jude 6; Rev 6:17; 16:14.

91 As Saviour: Matt 24:30-31; Phil 3:20-21; Heb 9:28; Tit 2:13. As Judge: Matt 7:21-23; 13:40-42; 16:27; 25:31-46; John 5:22-23, 27-29; Acts 10:42; 17:30-31; Rom 2:16; 1 Cor 4:5; 2 Thess 1:7-10; 2 Tim 4:1, 8; Jas 5:7-9; Rev 19:11; 22:12.

92 Matt 13:43; 24:30-31; 25:31; Rom 8:16-21; Col 3:4; 1 Thess 2:12; 4:14-17; 2 Thess 1:9-10; 2:1, 8, 14; 2 Tim 4:18; 1 Pet 1:3-5; 2 Pet 1:10-11; 1 John 3:2-3.

93 1 Cor 3:8, 12-14; 9:24-27; 1 Tim 6:12-15; 2 Tim 4:1-2, 7-8; 1 Pet 5:2-4; Rev 2:10; 3:11; 22:12.

94 Luke 8:11, 15; 13:6-9; John 15:16; Acts 20:24; 28:30-31; 1 Cor 15:58; 1 Tim 4:13- 16; 6:11-14; 2 Tim 1:13-14; 2:14-15, 22; 3:14; 4:2.

unshakeable foundation and focused on a glorious destination. So what is it like to serve God and his gospel in this in-between time? That is what we must now consider.

Worth pondering ...

The Son of God has his kingdom alone; there is none but he. Truth it is that it does not now appear to our eyes ... [but] in the end God will show us that he alone is Emperor, not only of heaven but also of earth, and that he has all in his hands, and that whatever at this day seems to be glorious is nothing but smoke, ... things that perish and have an end. And seeing that this is so, let us go on to serve God ... And though the worldlings persuade themselves nowadays that they are happy, and mock us as though we were fools and idiots, yet in the end God will show that he has not called us to his service to deceive us but he will make us partakers of that glory which he has given to our Lord Jesus Christ.[95]

[The] mighty Christ-event has given a new center to time, and so ... it is no longer the Parousia but rather the cross and resurrection of Christ that constitute the middle point and meaning of all that occurs... That which has already happened offers the solid guarantee for that which will take place. The hope of the final victory is so much the more vivid because of the unshakably firm conviction that the battle that decides the victory has already taken place... The present period of the Church is the time between the decisive battle, which has already occurred, and the "Victory Day."[96]

Jesus Christ [is] the foundation of eschatology... [and] the structure of eschatology, reaching the goal of God for us, in us, and with us... What he does for us, he does chiefly during his first coming in his crucifixion and resurrection. What he does in us, he does chiefly in his work through the Holy Spirit in the interim between the ascension and second advent. What he does with us, he does chiefly at his return... We usually begin the scope of eschatology too late; since Christ is the eschatos, eschatology begins with his incarnation, crucifixion, and resurrection.[97]

[A] Christian theology of history ... [gives] an understanding of the order of events in the divine programme. First, Jesus returned to heaven (Ascension). Secondly, the Holy Spirit came (Pentecost). Thirdly, the church goes out to witness (Mission). Fourthly, Jesus will come back (Parousia)... between the

---

[95] John Calvin, Sermons on the Epistles to Timothy & Titus (Banner of Truth, 1983 [1579]), 619-620 [on 1 Tim 6:13-16]. (I have updated the spelling and some of the wording.)
[96] Oscar Cullmann, Christ and Time: The Primitive Christian Conception of Time and History (SCM, 1951), 86, 87, 145 (his italics).
[97] Adrio König, The Eclipse of Christ in Eschatology: Toward a Christ-Centered Approach (Eerdmans, 1989), 64, 81 (his italics).

ascension and the Parousia, the disappearance and the reappearance of Jesus, there stretches a period of unknown length which is to be filled with the church's world-wide, Spirit-empowered witness to him. We need to hear the implied message of the angels: 'You have seen him go. You will see him come. But between that going and coming there must be another. The Spirit must come, and you must go—into the world for Christ.'[98]

---

[98] John R.W. Stott, The Message of Acts: To the Ends of the Earth, BST (IVP, 1990), 51.

2. Christian ministry is determined by God's work

2.3. Our work is framed by God's work

2.3.1. we serve between the comings of Jesus: his past completed work and his future completing work

2.3.2. so Christian ministry is tough[99]

This is because of our enemies—the world, the flesh, the devil;[100] because of our many weaknesses;[101] because of our sinfulness;[102] and because of the sins of others.[103] In the New Testament, the three greatest areas of failure are truth (false teaching), love (division), and holiness (immorality).

The Bible makes it clear to us that Christian ministry is tough going. Think of the story the book of Acts tells us about the unstoppable progress of the gospel. This is also a story of the many hardships faced by those who are spreading the gospel. More often than not, their ministries are dangerous and land them in serious trouble. They are threatened and abused, hounded from one place to another, attacked and flogged, unjustly charged and imprisoned, and even martyred. Why is there so much suffering in this story? Does ministry really have to be this hard?

The chief reason is that Christian discipleship—living for Jesus while we wait for his coming—is not easy. In following Jesus the Servant-Lord, the pathway we must take is marked by the cross (Luke 9:23-24; 14:27).[104] Like him, we must be willing to accept suffering and make sacrifices as the cost of our commitment to the will of God. Our journey into the kingdom of God takes us through many hardships (Acts 14:22). So it is

---

99 2 Cor 4:7-11; 6:3-10; 2 Tim 3:10-11.
100 Mark 13:9-13; John 15:18-21; 16:2; Eph 6:10-12; 1 Pet 5:8-9; 1 John 2:15-17.
101 Mark 14:29-31, 38; 2 Cor 4:7-11, 16; 11:29; 12:5, 9-10; 13:4.
102 Acts 20:28, 30-31; Rom 6:12-13; 1 Cor 9:27; 1 Tim 5:20; Jas 3:1-2; 1 Pet 2:11.
103 Rom 16:17-18; 1 Thess 2:14-16; 2 Thess 3:2; 2 Tim 3:8-9; 4:10, 14-15; Tit 1:10- 14; 2 Pet 2:1-3; 3 John 9-11; Jude 3-4, 16-19.
104 Luke 9:23-24; 14:27; John 12:24-26.

not surprising that the Bible likens the Christian life to warfare.[105] The same is true of Christian ministry.[106] So the hardships we face in ministry should not be surprising. They are not something new, but an inescapable part of living for Jesus in this in-between time. That is why, when Paul refers to the sufferings he endured in his ministry (2 Tim 3:10-11), he immediately goes on to note that "everyone who wants to live a godly life in Christ Jesus will be persecuted" (2 Tim 3:12).

This brings us to a second reason why ministry is difficult. As in a war, we face hostile opposition, just as Jesus did. Although this is part-and-parcel of our Christian commitment, this opposition is intensified by our involvement in Christian ministry.[107] The devil's fiercest attacks are on those in the front-line of the battle, so Christ's soldiers should expect to undergo suffering (2 Tim 2:3). The weapons he uses are error and terror, fraud and force. That is why Jesus calls him a liar and a murderer (John 8:44). He disguises himself as an angel of light (2 Cor 11:14), and he preys upon us like a roaring lion (1 Pet 5:8). So we will find him misleading and mistreating, using both trickery and tyranny. This means that we will meet opposition in the church as well as in the world.

The internal opposition is most likely to come from unfaithful leaders who pervert the gospel and unconverted religious people who find the gospel offensive. The opposition we meet outside the church varies from one society to another. It ranges along a spectrum, from a stubborn determination to ignore the Christian message through scornful dismissal of it and all who believe it or censorship intended to silence it all the way to violence and murder. The mortal danger facing our brothers and sisters in some parts of the world far outweighs the annoyance or mockery Western Christians might have to bear—but our innate desire for acceptance and approval makes any opposition difficult to cope with. Yet I must be ready for it: if I am involved in Christian ministry, I will have to "set my face like flint" (Isa 50:7).

There is a third reason why Christian ministry is tough going. That is because we are all weak and vulnerable and prone to go astray. This is

---

[105] Luke 14:31-33; Rom 13:12; Eph 6:11-17; 1 Thess 5:8.
[106] 2 Cor 6:7; 10:3-4; Phil 2:25; 1 Tim 1:18; 2 Tim 2:3; Phm 2.
[107] Luke 21:12-17; Jn 15:18-21; 16:1-2; 17:11-12, 14-15; 1 Cor 16:9; 1 Thess 2:2, 14-16; 2 Tim 4:15.

why we find it hard to resist the unrelenting pressures applied by the world, the flesh, and the devil. As we have just noted, it is not easy to stand firm against the assaults of our enemy, the patron of error and terror. Nor is it easy to withstand the hostility of the world around us. But here we are thinking of the problems created by the flesh, our innate sinfulness. We will often see this powerful tendency at work in those we serve and also those with whom we serve. As a result, we must be realistic, not expecting that our service will always be welcomed or that others will never fail. But we do not need to look at other people to see the flesh on display, as it will be all too evident in our own self-centred and self-seeking ways. This is why we struggle to accept the sufferings that come our way in life and ministry. This is why we are reluctant to make sacrifices. And this is why we must be vigilant, never underestimating the tenacity of our sinfulness: "if you think you are standing firm, be careful that you don't fall!" (1 Cor 10:12). Christian ministry is difficult because it is always to the sinful - and always by the sinful!

Something else that makes our ministry tough is the fact that is never finished. As we wait for the Lord to bring his saving work to its glorious completion, there is always more that could be done—more people to be reached with the gospel; more growth to be seen in those who are believers; more resources to be created and more workers recruited and trained so that the gospel keeps making progress; and so on. Yet our abilities and energies are limited, so that we are not capable of adding more and more all the time. This makes it vital that we keep reminding ourselves that the work is the Lord's—and he is well aware that we are frail and flawed instruments: "he remembers that we are dust" (Psa 103:14).

We must also learn to live within limits, accepting that none of our work is ever perfect. We have to be content with doing the best we can do in the circumstances. Yes, this sermon would be much better if I could spend another week on it—but Sundays reappear relentlessly, every seven days! So if I have done my best, I can trust God to use a far-from-perfect effort for his good purposes. And even if I haven't done my best—by being lazy or foolish in my use of time, for example—I can trust him to forgive me and also to have mercy on my hearers. The Lord we serve can feed a multitude with just a couple of buns and fish!

Christian ministry is not for the fainthearted! It is tough going and requires lots of grit on our part. It is therefore essential that we know why we must stay the course and also how to keep on keeping on. There is only one way to learn this: we must go back to the foundations again and again. We must fix our eyes on Jesus the Servant-Lord, never tiring of remembering all that he endured for us (2 Thess 3:5; Heb 12:1-3). We must also keep sinking our roots deeper and deeper into the grace of God. The way to become more steadfast in our ministries is to stay grounded in his steadfast love: grit grows best in the soil of grace. We must keep reminding ourselves that Christian ministry is a great privilege, a gift from a generous God. And we must stay focused on the glory that is coming. Because it involves many hardships, ministry will often lead to tears—but on that Day our gracious God will wipe away every one of those tears (Rev 7:17; 21:4). If I am to finish the race, I must keep returning to these great truths.

Worth pondering ...

Take heed to yourselves, because the tempter will more ply you with his temptations than other men... He beareth the greatest malice to those that are engaged to do him the greatest mischief. As he hateth Christ more than any of us ... so doth he hate the leaders under him, more than the common soldiers: he knows what a rout he may make among them, if the leaders fall before their eyes... O what a conquest will he think he hath got, if he can make a minister lazy and unfaithful, if he can tempt a minister into covetousness or scandal![108]

[Paul] recommends Epaphroditus ... [as] his fellow-soldier, by which word he expresses the condition of the ministers of the Gospel, in that they are engaged in an incessant warfare, for Satan will not allow them to promote the Gospel without a conflict. Let those, then, who prepare themselves for edifying the Church, know that war is declared against them and already prepared. This, indeed, is common to all Christians, to serve in the camp of Christ; for Satan is the enemy of all. It is, however, more particularly applicable to ministers of the Word, who lead the ranks and bear the standard.[109]

Since suffering is a necessary, normal and expected part of faithful Christian leadership, the quality leaders need most is I.C.F.D. This stands for Incredible Capacity for Disappointment.[110]

Christ's subjects are the world's rebels, and if they will not forfeit their allegiance to Christ, the world will fall upon them... Now the ministers of all ages are mustered and enrolled for the same war with the prophets and apostles; we maintain the same cause ... and we expect the same crown; why should we grudge to drink of the same cup?[111]

---

[108] Richard Baxter, The Reformed Pastor (Banner of Truth, 1974 [1656]), 74, 75.

[109] John Calvin, Calvin's New Testament Commentaries (Eerdmans, 1965 [1556]), 11.263 [on Phil 2:25].

[110] Brian J. Dodd, Empowered Church Leadership: Ministry in the Spirit according to Paul (IVP, 2003), 75.

[111] Thomas Manton, Complete Works (Maranatha, n.d.), 10.365, 367.

2. Christian ministry is determined by God's work

2.3. Our work is framed by God's work

2.3.1. we serve between the comings of Jesus: his past completed work and his future completing work

2.3.3. so Christian workers must be accountable

We should be accountable to our fellow-believers.[112] We are accountable primarily to the Lord, who will judge our ministries.[113]

Ministry is not for mavericks! The gospel is not a licence that frees us to do whatever we want however we like. In ministry we are not owners but stewards, not masters but servants—and so we are answerable to the Lord who gives us our ministries for what we do in them. We are also more vulnerable to sin than we often realize. As a result, we could easily end up failing badly. That is why we need to be accountable to our fellow-believers.

At one level, this is part of the "one another" dimension of the Christian life—which refers to all of the ways the New Testament tells us we should interact with each other.[114] Of special importance here is our responsibility to encourage and exhort each other to be true to the Lord and to our calling to be his holy people.[115] This kind of mutual ministry is done most effectively when we meet regularly in small groups and pray for each other. As we get to know each other better and trust each other more, we can be more open about our struggles and weaknesses—and

---

[112] Matt 18:15-17; Acts 14:26-27; Gal 6:1-2; 2 Thess 3:14-15; 1 Tim 3:10; 4:15-16; 5:19-20; Jas 5:19-20.

[113] Rom 14:10-12; 1 Cor 3:8, 12-15; 4:4-5; 2 Cor 5:9-10; 10:18; 1 Thess 2:3-5; Heb 13:17; Jas 3:1; Rev 2:20-23.

[114] John 13:34-35; 15:12; Rom 12:10, 16; 13:8; 14:13, 19; 15:5, 7, 14; 16:16; 1 Cor 12:25; Gal 5:13; 6:2; Eph 4:2, 32; 5:21; Phil 2:3; Col 3:9, 13; 1 Thess 3:12; 4:9, 18; 5:11, 15; 2 Thess 1:3; Heb 10:24; Jas 5:16; 1 Pet 1:22; 4:9; 5:5; 1 John 1:7; 3:11, 23; 4:7, 11- 12; 2 John 5.

[115] Rom 1:7; 1 Cor 1:2; Eph 4:1, 17-24; 5:3-16; 1 Thess 4:7; 1 Pet 1:14-16.

this enables us to give each other the right blend of encouragements and reminders, warnings and rebukes, sympathy and support.

Mutual accountability is also meant to be part of leadership in the local church, which in the New Testament is always a shared responsibility.[116] Our suitability for any ministry position we aspire to has to be assessed by the appropriate people (1 Tim 3:2-12). If those who appoint us are wise, they will put in place regular opportunities to review how we are going in our ministry. And if we are wise, we will face the fact that our sinfulness makes us vulnerable, and so will put in place measures that make it as difficult as possible for sin to bring us undone. One of the most important is honest and open relationships with people who will keep me accountable.

Sadly, even our best efforts do not always succeed in keeping sin at bay, and people in ministry positions sometimes make terrible choices and do great wrong. These failures often stem from the corrupting effects of money or power or sex. Whenever they happen, the church and its leaders must exercise the appropriate discipline, which may need to involve dismissing the offender from their position. This discipline must reflect both the holiness of God and the grace of God, who hates and judges all sin and yet forgives and restores every penitent sinner. So our response to what has occurred must not be too mild, as though it is not serious, or too severe, implying that there is no way back for the offender.[117] We should be aiming at their restoration—a process that begins with a repentance that demonstrates its genuineness by admitting the sin involved and renouncing it, by doing everything possible to right whatever wrong has been done, and by accepting closer supervision if and when it is appropriate for the person to resume their ministry.

The most important reason for taking all of this seriously is the fact that we are answerable to the Lord. The Lord we are serving is to be our Judge: on the last day, we will stand before him to give an account of our lives and ministries.[118] But there is an important sense in which this is

---

[116] Acts 11:25; 13:1; 14:23; 20:17, 28; 1 Cor 16:15-16; Phil 1:1; 1 Thess 5:12-13; 1 Tim 5:17.
[117] Matt 18:15-17; 1 Cor 5:1-5,9-13; 2 Cor 2:5-8; Gal 6:1-2; 2 Thess 3:11-15; 1 Tim 5:19-20.
[118] Rom 14:10; 2 Cor 5:10; Rev 20:12.

true every day: all that we do now is done before him, in his presence.[119] We should therefore keep reminding ourselves that God is our witness and that he tests our hearts.[120] The best way of preparing for the judgment that awaits us at the End is to give proper weight to the fact that our ministries are subject to his scrutiny every day.

The certainty of the judgment to come should shape the conduct of our ministries in various ways. Important among them is the fact that since the Lord is the one to whom we must give an account, no one else has any right to pass final judgment on us (1 Cor 4:3-5). It is true that we are to be the servants of God's people—but they are not to be our masters. Our accountability to other believers should be real, but it is not absolute. We must set ourselves to please and obey the Lord in every situation— and this will sometimes mean that other people will not be pleased with us. But if we have to make a choice, it is obvious that our loyalty must always belong to him: "If I were still trying to please people, I would not be a servant of Christ" (Gal 1:10).

The coming judgment also means that the true worth of our service is not evident in the here and now. In part, this is due to the fact that the fruits of what we do are often unseen and unknown. There can be a long gap between sowing-time and harvest-time—and sometimes there just doesn't seem to be a harvest at all. So there is an important sense in which we serve now by faith and not by sight. We must keep doing what is right, trusting God to use our work as only he can. Not knowing the true worth of our service now is also due to the fact that it is not measured by the standards of the world, but by the Lord. When he brings what is hidden from us into the open (1 Cor 4:5), there are likely to be some surprises. What looks to us like success may turn out to have serious flaws—and what seems small and insignificant may prove to be solid gold. If there are any front-row seats in the kingdom of heaven, most of them will probably be filled by little old ladies who went largely unnoticed (by us!) but who kept praying faithfully and serving quietly.

---

[119] Acts 10:33; 2 Cor 2:17; 7:12; Gal 1:20; 1 Thess 1:3; 3:9; 5:27; 2 Tim 2:14; 4:1; Heb 4:13; Jas 4:10; 1 John 3:19, 21.
[120] Jer 17:10; Rom 1:9; 1 Thess 2:4-5, 10; Rev 2:23.

There are many temptations and pitfalls around us and many weaknesses within us. This combination can easily bring us undone! We should therefore remind ourselves frequently of two important facts: that every day we live and serve in the presence of God, and that on the last day we will stand before his judgment seat. We should also ensure that our lives and ministries are subject to scrutiny by believers who can be trusted to warn us of danger, to rebuke us for doing wrong, and to encourage us to get back on track and stay true. As we serve in this in-between time, we cannot afford to be beyond criticism. If we are to stay faithful, we need to be accountable.

Worth pondering ...

Men...may condemn when they should commend, and applaud what they should neglect and avoid; but the judgment of God is according to truth. He never rewards but upon just reason, and he ever rewards in proportion to the diligence and faithfulness of his servants... Faithful servants, when they are ill used by men, should encourage themselves in God. And it is to God, the chief agent and director of the great work of the gospel, to whom those that labour with him should endeavour to approve themselves. They are always under his eye...[121]

[Whereas] some depend on the opinions of men and weigh themselves in the false balance of public opinion and others are deceived by their own arrogance, Paul bids us care for only one kind of glory, namely that we should please the Lord by whose judgment we stand or fall...let us make it our one aim to win God's approval and let us be content with His approbation alone, since by right it should be regarded as worth more than all the applauses of the whole world.[122]

[Pastors] are not owners, but stewards; they are not sovereigns, but servants. There is a "great Shepherd of the sheep"...to whom they must give an account of their office, of their work, and of the flock committed to their charge.[123]

What a mean and beggarly thing it is for a man only to do his work well when he is watched. Such oversight is for boys at school and mere hirelings...the true Christian wants no eye of man to watch him...There is about a real Christian a prevailing sense that God sees him, and he does not care who else may set his eye upon him; it is enough for him that God is there. He hath small respect to the eye of man, he neither courts nor dreads it...This is to be a true servant of Christ; to escape from being an eyeservant to men by...working ever beneath the eye of God.[124]

---

[121] Simon Browne in Matthew Henry, Commentary on the Whole Bible (Hendrickson, 2008 [1721]), 1799.
[122] John Calvin, Calvin's New Testament Commentaries (Eerdmans, 1964 [1547]), 10.137, 138 [on 2 Cor 10:17-18].
[123] John Owen, An Exposition of the Epistle to the Hebrews (Banner of Truth, 1991 [1684]), 7.466.
[124] C.H. Spurgeon, Counsel for Christian Workers (Christian Focus, 2001), 66-67.

2. Christian ministry is determined by God's work

2.3. Our work is framed by God's work

2.3.1. we serve between the comings of Jesus: his past completed work and his future completing work

2.3.4. so Christian ministry is glorious

We are given the privilege of being God's coworkers, doing "the work of the Lord".[125] This work cannot fail,[126] and its fruit will be eternal and glorious.[127]

Ministry in this in-between time does not come easily. We face determined opposition, and we have many weaknesses. Yet despite all our foes and all our faults, Christian service cannot fail. This is because we are serving the risen, exalted Lord, who rules at God's right hand—and his kingdom cannot fail. He is gathering his church from all the nations—and on the last day, his redeemed people will stand before him, an assembly too vast for anyone to number (Rev 7:9-10). Nothing can prevent him from completing this work, bringing his entire church to everlasting glory. This is because the decisive events on which our salvation depends have already taken place: because the D-day of Jesus' death and resurrection lies behind us, his final triumph is certain. All that remains is for him to bring to its glorious completion the salvation and the kingdom he has already secured. And out of his grace, he chooses to use us and our ministries as he does so. This gives us a very strong incentive to put everything we have into this work, for our labour will not—indeed it cannot—turn out to be wasted or fruitless (1 Cor 15:58). Because we are serving the redeeming, risen, ruling, and returning Lord, our ministries will bear eternal fruit.

---

[125] 1 Cor 3:9; 15:58; 16:10; 2 Cor 6:1; Phil 2:30; 1 Thess 3:2; 1 Tim 1:3.

[126] Isa 46:9-10; 55:10-11; John 6:39-40; 10:27-29; 1 Cor 1:8-9; 15:58; Phil 1:6; 1 Thess 5:23-24; Heb 12:28; 1 Pet 1:3-5; 5:10; Rev 7:9-10.

[127] John 17:5, 20-24; Rom 8:16-23; Eph 5:27; 1 Thess 2:19-20; 2 Thess 1:9- 10; 2:14; 2 Tim 4:8, 18; 1 Pet 5:1-4; Jude 1, 24-25; Rev 21:2-5, 23-26.

That our service cannot fail does not mean that we will find it easy. As we have noted, the Bible makes it clear that the work of the gospel is tough going. The world, the flesh, and the devil are unrelenting in their opposition, and it is not easy to remain steadfast in the face of such powerful foes. Nor does this mean that all of our service will be what it should be. We must guard against sloppy work and halfhearted efforts. We must watch our motives, so that we are not proud and self-seeking in what we do. We must take care that we do not build with wood, hay, or straw (1 Cor 3:12-13). We must resist the pressures to follow the ways of the world, and so on. Nor is there any guarantee that everything we attempt for God and the gospel will succeed. Particular ventures may fail because they were inadequately planned or poorly run. Even good ideas don't always work, and it isn't always obvious why that is. This is quite a long list of things we are saying—and there is more that could be added! So what do we mean by claiming that Christian ministry cannot fail?

This is not making a claim about us, as though we were indispensable or infallible. It is a way of recognizing the greatness and the grace of the Lord we are serving. This is what we see when we remember where we are and what we are doing. So where are we? Our ministries are located between Easter and the End. Because the Lord has already won the decisive victory at Easter, he will certainly complete his saving work at the End, bringing his whole church from every place and time into the glory of the new creation. His greatness is such that nothing can prevent him from doing this. And what are we doing in this in-between time? By his grace, we are involved in "the work of the Lord". Because he is good to us, he has given us a place in this great work, choosing to use what we do for him as he moves it to its glorious completion. With Easter as its foundation and the End as its destination, and with his work as its setting, our service cannot fail. So saying this is not shining a spotlight on us or making exaggerated claims about what we are capable of; it is telling us something important about the Lord we serve.

Such is his kindness that no matter how small or lowly it is, nothing we do for him will be overlooked or forgotten: even the cup of water will have its reward.[128] A crown of glory in his kingdom awaits all who have

---

[128] Matt 10:42; Mark 9:41; Eph 6:8; Heb 6:10.

loved and served him.[129] On that great day we will also get to see the fruit that has come from our ministries. The key to this is the word of God, which can never be fruitless and always accomplishes his saving purpose in people's lives.[130] That is why we must involve his word in our ministries in every way we can. None of that work will ever be in vain: its fruit will last.[131] And one reason for our wonder and praise on that day will be seeing how he has woven this fruit into the glory of his finished work.

Despite the flaws and limitations of even our best efforts, he will somehow incorporate it all into the fabric of his everlasting kingdom. The New Jerusalem will shine with the glory of God (Rev 21:10-11)—but it will also have room for "the glory and honour of the nations" (Rev 21:26). By the time we reach this amazing statement, Revelation has already made it clear that the nations are filled with all kinds of evil, and face terrible judgment for all the ways in which they have opposed God's rule and persecuted God's people.[132] So their glory and honour does not lie in anything they produce by their own resources and for their own ends. Nor is it anything that would be regarded as glorious by the unbelieving world. John is speaking about the fruit of the gospel. The glory of the nations is the church of God: the vast assembly of the redeemed from every nation that will gather before the Lord and the Lamb (Rev 7:9-10). Before they assembled before him, while they were dispersed among the nations, they lived to honour the Lamb who purchased them by his blood (Rev 5:9). This is what brings honour to the nations—and this is how that honour enters the city: everything the redeemed did for the Lamb will follow them into the city of God (Rev 14:13). So as we persevere in Christian ministry, each act of service, however humble, each day's work, however ordinary, is steadily adding to the glory that our nation will contribute to the city of God. On that great day we will finally get to see how truly beautiful and noble serving is—and what stunning glories God has made out of everything we have done for him.

---

[129] Matt 25:34; 1 Cor 9:25; 2 Tim 4:8; Heb 12:28; Jas 1:12; 2:5; 1 Pet 5:4; Rev 3:11.
[130] Isa 55:10-11; Acts 20:32; Rom 1:16.
[131] John 15:16; 1 Cor 15:58.
[132] Rev 13:7; 14:8; 16:19; 18:3, 23; 19:15; 20:7-9.

Could there be any greater incentive to stay true and work hard? We are serving a Lord whose glorious purpose cannot be frustrated or defeated, a Lord who makes room for us and includes us in the magnificent work that he is doing, a Lord who will honour everything we have done for him (Matt 25:21, 23). The more often we bring this into focus, the more likely we are to stand firm and give ourselves unstintingly to the work of the Lord (1 Cor 15:58). With Easter behind us and the End ahead of us, with the Lord above us and his Spirit within us, why would we want to hold back or give up?

Worth pondering ...

[Whether] we look to Moses or the prophets, to Christ or his apostles, still we shall find that the persecutions, afflictions and bonds of God's saints rather further than hinder the gospel, rather make for than against the increase of Christ's kingdom on earth, rather help than hurt the church. But how does this come to pass? The adversaries of God's saints intend no such thing. No indeed, their whole desire and endeavor in troubling and persecuting the saints of God is to make havoc of the church and to hinder or abolish the gospel of Jesus Christ. How then? ... such is the power of Christ that however their enemies do band themselves against his saints to work the subversion of the gospel and the truth of Christ Jesus, yet he can at his pleasure, and does, make their devices to be of no effect—not only so, but turns them to the very opposite end than what they had imagined.[133]

Though none of God's servants can deserve any thing from him, though there be much that is blamable even in their best services, yet shall their fidelity be commended and crowned by him; and should they be condemned, reproached, or vilified, by their fellow-servants, he will roll away all such unjust censures and reproaches...[134]

[Inasmuch] as God causes the doctrine which we proclaim to prosper, even if we never see its effect with our eyes, let us continue to perform our office and persevere in our calling. When the seed is sown it sinks hidden into the soil, but at the appropriate time it produces its fruit. Correspondingly, our Lord labors in such a way that when we preach his Word, some of it will always bear fruit, as God so blesses our labor as to lift it above frustration... Let us realize, therefore, that although for the most part we may judge our preaching to be ineffective, and even to arouse great evil, we are, nevertheless, to remember that God approves of the preaching of his Gospel.[135]

We are labouring for eternity, and we count not our work by each day's advance, as men measure theirs; it is God's work, and must be measured by His standard. Be ye well assured that, when time, and things created, and all that oppose themselves to the Lord's truth, shall be gone, every earnest

---

[133] Henry Airay in Graham Tomlin (ed), Philippians, Colossians, RCS: NT XI (IVP Academic, 2013), 20-21.

[134] Simon Browne in Matthew Henry's Commentary on the Whole Bible (Hendrickson, 2008 [1721]), 1801 [on 1 Cor 4:5].

[135] John Calvin, Sermons on the Book of Micah (P&R, 2003 [1551]), 369f.

sermon preached, and every importunate prayer offered, and every form of Christian service honestly rendered, shall remain embedded in the mighty structure which God from all eternity has resolved to raise to His own honour.[136]

---

[136] C.H. Spurgeon in Larry J. Michael, Spurgeon on Leadership: Key Insights for Christian Leaders from the Prince of Preachers (Kregel, 2010), 95.

Part 3: THE SOURCE OF CHRISTIAN MINISTRY

3. Christian ministry is dependent on God's gifts

3.1. God equips us to serve him.[1]

We have already considered the most important thing we need to know about Christian ministry. This is the fact that we have a ministry only because God is immensely kind to us. He is at work bringing in his great salvation and establishing his eternal kingdom. In this work, he is not dependent on us—and we are not necessary to him. Yet he makes room for us in his work, conferring on us the great dignity of being his co-workers. Christian ministry is a gift from "the God of all grace" (1 Pet 5:10). But we meet this wonderfully generous God before we receive the gift of ministry from him. The first and most fundamental gift we must receive is the utterly amazing, totally undeserved, and desperately needed gift of salvation. He calls us into his salvation before he calls us into his service. We become his dearly loved children before we become his greatly privileged co-workers. The gift of ministry comes after the gift of new life.

While it is important to distinguish them, we need to recognize that these two gifts are closely connected. This becomes clear when we consider how we receive the gift of salvation. New life is possible only because Jesus died for us—and by his death he has purchased us, so that we now belong to him.[2] In saving us, he has bought us and set us free to serve him.[3] We enter this new life by confessing Jesus as Lord.[4] This is personal as well as universal: he is not just the Lord, Lord of all; he is also my Lord. And because he is our Lord, we are his slaves, meant to serve him.[5] So we live out our new life as servants under the rule of Jesus the

---

[1] Rom 12:6-8; 1 Cor 1:4-7; 12:7; Eph 4:7; 1 Tim 4:14; 2 Tim 1:6; 1 Pet 4:10.
[2] Acts 20:28; 1 Cor 6:19-20; 7:23; Tit 2:14; Rev 5:9.
[3] Rom 6:16-18, 22; 1 Pet 2:16; Rev 1:5-6.
[4] Acts 2:36; 16:31; Rom 10:9-13; Col 2:6.
[5] Luke 12:35-38, 42-44; 17:7-10; John 13:16; 15:20; Acts 20:19; Rom 1:1; 12:11; 14:18; 16:18; 1 Cor 3:5; 4:1; 7:22; Gal 1:10; Phil 1:1; Col 3:24; 4:12; 2 Tim 2:24; Jas 1:1; 1 Pet 1:2; 2 Pet 1:1; Jude 1; Rev 1:1; 2:20.

Lord. In this sense, we can say that we are saved to serve. Inside the gift of salvation we receive the gift of ministry.

God's great generosity does not stop with the gift of ministry. He does not call us into his service and then abandon us, leaving us to struggle through on our own. This would be a crushing burden, for we are not capable of doing God's work: we cannot give sight to the blind and life to the dead; we cannot change people and make them fit to be with God forever in his kingdom. But "the God of all grace" does not treat his servants like this. Along with the gift of ministry, he also confers on us gifts for ministry: God not only gives us the great privilege of serving him, he also equips us to do so. The most fundamental way he does this is by giving us his Spirit. So, as we learned in our discussion of 2.1.2 above, in all of our work for God we must depend on the Spirit of God. But God's grace goes even further than this, for the Spirit not only empowers us but also gifts us. God not only gives us the gift of his Spirit; he also gives us gifts by his Spirit.[6] These gifts equip us to serve the Lord (1 Cor 12:4-5).

What does the Bible teach us about these gifts? We will work our way through the most important truths over the next few pages, but there are three that deserve special mention. The first comes from the fact that the New Testament does not use any of the normal Greek words for "gift" here. The word that it does use (*charisma*) indicates that we are meant to see them as specific expressions and displays of grace (*charis*). That is why New Testament references to these gifts often make an explicit connection with God's grace.[7] This is yet another way in which God displays his great kindness and generosity to his church. And because we know that his grace is so rich and lavish, we can be confident that no one will miss out on these gifts—and that the gifts won't all be the same.

Secondly, each gift is to be understood as a "manifestation of the Spirit" (1 Cor 12:7). That is, it enables us to see the unseen Spirit at work (1 Cor 12:11). And what kind of work does he do? It is often assumed that we should expect his work to be "supernatural". This is the right answer if we mean that it is something that only God could do. But it is a mistake to assume that whatever God does will be spectacular and abnormal, the

---

[6]   1 Cor 12:4, 7, 11; 14:1, 12; Heb 2:4.
[7]   Rom 12:6; 1 Cor 1:4-7; Eph 4:7-8, 11-12.

kind of thing that doesn't normally happen. That is certainly true of some of his work—but what about the work he does in us and through us as we serve him day to day (1 Cor 12:4-6)? Does this have to be extraordinary in order to be what the Spirit is doing?

The way we serve is usually based on what we are good at. These abilities are part of what we are as individuals: the particular mix of traits and aptitudes we received at conception. We know that God is behind this as the author and giver of all our abilities—which even unbelievers acknowledge unconsciously by referring to people who are very talented as "gifted"! So what could be more natural than the God who made us harnessing and using for his work what he has built into us? Why should the Spirit need to bypass our nature or even override it in order to get his work done? It would not be strange if he sometimes heightens what is there already, to make it more powerful and effective. And he might sometimes give us a new capacity we did not have before—and at least some of these could well be quite exceptional and extraordinary, as they were in Corinth (1 Cor 12:9-10). But some of these "manifestations of the Spirit" will turn out to be skills and abilities we have had all our lives, now dedicated to God's service and given by his Spirit the power and effectiveness they need to bear fruit for God.

Thirdly, we have these gifts not as owners but as "stewards" (1 Pet 4:10). The overriding responsibility of stewards, entrusted with something they don't own, is to be faithful (1 Cor 4:2). This means that we must not squander what God has given us, either by leaving it in cold storage (Matt 25:24-25) or by using it for our own ends (Acts 8:18-23). Instead, we must make the most of all the opportunities for service that we get or can create. What God has given us is meant to be put to work: the way to be faithful in our stewardship is to make as much use as possible of our gifts. And Peter makes it very clear what our aim must be in all of this: "... so that in all things God may be praised through Jesus Christ. To him be the glory ..." (1 Pet 4:11). What we receive from God's grace must always and only be used for God's glory.

God is an amazingly kind and generous giver. He shows immense kindness in making room for us and giving us a place in the work he is doing. And then he displays even more kindness by equipping us thoroughly for this service. He gives us the privilege of serving him and he also makes us able to do so. The gift of ministry should make us eager to serve—and knowing that God gifts us for ministry should mean that we don't hold back. We can put all we've got into our ministries, because we know that he will give us all that we need.

Worth pondering ...

[The] Lord has provided you with such gifts and talents as are needful for the work to which He has commissioned you ... What manner of person would you be if you either would allow these wondrous benefits, talents, opportunities, and esteem to be unused, or if you were to display them proudly, seeking to attain worldly honor with spiritual benefits? They are too precious for this. Acknowledge therefore their preciousness and may you burn with zeal to use them for that purpose for which they have been given, namely, to serve your Lord and to be beneficial to His church.[8]

[Peter] would have the Spirit's gifts used in the service of others, and admonishes Christians to consider all they have as given of God. The heathen have no such thought, but live as if life and all they possess were of their own attaining. But let Christians know they are under obligation to serve God with their gifts; and God is served when they employ them for the advantage and service of the people—reforming them, bringing them to a knowledge of God, and thus building up, strengthening, and perpetuating the Church. Of such love the world knows nothing at all.[9]

Whatever excellency you have, or however you are dignified from others, are not all these things the free gifts of God? And should you boast of that which is God's free gift, and of which you are but receivers ... The glory belongeth not to the party receiving, but to the person giving. Therefore we should not rob God of his glory ... As we have nothing but from God, so we should have nothing but for God. All the gifts you have you receive from him, and not from yourselves; and therefore you must use them for him, and not for yourselves.[10]

---

8   Wilhelmus à Brakel, The Christian's Reasonable Service (Reformation Heritage, 1993 [1700]), 2.153.
9   Martin Luther, Sermons (Baker, 1983), 7.323 [on 1 Pet 4:10].
10 Thomas Manton, Complete Works (Maranatha, n.d.), 16.365.

3. Christian ministry is dependent on God's gifts

3.2. There are many different ministry gifts.

3.2.1. all are important and all are necessary.

Christian ministry is only for the gifted—and all of God's people are gifted! Everyone who has been brought into his great salvation has also been given a place in his service: we have all been given the privilege of working for him. And we have all been given the gifts we need to play our part in what God is doing.

We have learned that each gift (*charisma*) is a particular instance of God's grace (*charis*). And here we see how rich his grace is, for these gifts are distributed to each one of us.[11] No one is overlooked; no one misses out. Every believer is gifted for the work of service; each of us has something to contribute to the building up of the church (Eph 4:12). As a result, none of us is dispensable. No one can afford to be a passenger, because every part is needed for the effective functioning of the body: the foot as well as the hand; the ear as well as the eye (1 Cor 12:15-17). By the same token, no one should be undervalued or written off. Every part of the body is needed: the hand as well as the eye, the feet as well as the head (1 Cor 12:21-22).

All alike are gifted—but not gifted alike. The richness of God's grace is seen not only in its spread but also in its diversity. He has equipped us in many different ways—so Peter compares his grace to a "multi-coloured" garment (the literal meaning of the word he uses in 1 Pet 4:10). A church is like the human body, composed of many different parts.[12] And like a body, it is both one and many. It has unity without uniformity, since all of us are different as a result of the Spirit's gifting work (1 Cor 12:5, 7, 11). It also has diversity without division, since all of us are one in Christ as a result of the Spirit's baptizing work (Rom 12:5; 1 Cor 12:13). So we are not like an army parade, all dressed the same and

---

[11]   Rom 12:6; 1 Cor 12:7, 11; Eph 4:7; 1 Pet 4:10.
[12]   Rom 12:4; 1 Cor 12:12, 14, 20.

indistinguishable from each other, but like a choir, with our differences blended together in harmony.

In view of the richness of God's grace, we should not have too narrow or restricted a view of ministry-gifts. One way of making this mistake is to focus on the spectacular and extraordinary. This seems to be what Paul is trying to counter in 1 Corinthians 12–14, which suggests that at least some members of that church had a quite lopsided view of how the Spirit of God does his work. They apparently believed that the more out of the ordinary and out of our control something was, the more spiritual it was. The result was that they concentrated on just a few gifts, especially tongues and miraculous powers. Paul has to tell them that the true test of whether activities and experiences come from the Spirit is not their force but their focus and their fruit.

The first and most important marker of the Spirit's presence and work is an unwavering focus on the Lord Jesus. That is because the heart of his mission, his overriding goal in everything he does, is to glorify Jesus (John 16:14). So the Spirit is not there whenever Jesus is rejected and not honoured, no matter how overwhelmed and overwhelming a speaker is. Conversely, the Spirit is at work whenever Jesus is confessed and honoured, no matter how ordinary and unspectacular the speaker or the occasion (1 Cor 12:3). The Corinthians should have known this, because before they were converted they had experienced spiritual powers—but these were obviously not from God, because they had led them away from him into idolatry (1 Cor 12:2).

The second crucial marker of the Spirit's work is its fruit. Whatever the Spirit does is aimed at the growth and upbuilding of all believers: his gifts are for the common good (1 Cor 12:7). The greatest work he does is not working miracles through us but growing love in us (1 Cor 13:1–14:1). Where love is absent, so is the Spirit—no matter how many marvels or displays of apparently supernatural power occur (1 Cor 13:1-2).

There is a third principle Paul has to teach this church. The Spirit's work is not confined to a few spectacular powers but is displayed in a wide range of gifts: "the body is not made up of one part but of many" (1 Cor 12:14, 20). Some of these may be extraordinary and even miraculous— but the Spirit's work is seen in everything that is Christ-honouring and church-building, even very ordinary and unremarkable gifts. So Paul seems to have made some additions to this church's list of spiritual gifts, to subvert the way they were looking at the Spirit's work. He begins the list with two important but unspectacular contributions to church life: saying wise or knowledgeable things (1 Cor 12:8).[13] When he comes back to the list, he starts it another way: "God has placed in the church first of all apostles …" (1 Cor 12:28). This is a way of saying that the basis of the church's life is the gospel—so the Corinthians' primary and constant focus should not be the ongoing work of the Spirit but the once-for-all work of the Son.[14] And the words that should matter most to them are not those of tongues-speakers but the Spirit-taught words in which Paul teaches them about the work and will of God.[15] Then in the middle of those gifts that seem to have attracted them most, Paul inserts "gifts … of helping, of guidance" (1 Cor 12:28). These are quite ordinary, but contributions the church always needs—and likely to be included in what the Spirit enabled Timothy, Apollos, and the household of Stephanas to do for this church.[16]

So the Corinthians must not think that everything that is overwhelming or out-of-the-ordinary comes from the Spirit. They must learn to see his work in everything that centres upon Jesus and his gospel and that expresses and promotes love, and also in every activity that contributes to the health and growth of the church.

There is another way of taking too narrow a view of ministry-gifts. This is bound up with the view that I have to discover what my gift is before I know what ministry I should take on. This implies that there is a fixed and limited number of gifts, that I or we have some way of knowing what they are and discerning which of them has been allocated to me, and that I will only ever have one of these gifts. But the lists in the

---

13   The KJV's "the word of wisdom" and "the word of knowledge" makes them sound like names for special gifts, whereas Paul most likely means everyday gifts: "wise words" and "knowledgeable words".
14   1 Cor 1:17; 2:1-7; 3:10-11; 4:15; 9:1-2; 15:1-2.
15   1 Cor 2:12-13; 14:6, 18-19, 37.
16   1 Cor 16:10, 12, 15-16.

New Testament don't give the impression of a limited pool of gifts that is unchanging.[17]

And do gifts come before ministries—or do they come with them? We are normally surrounded by many needs and opportunities for Christian service. When no one else is doing something that should be done, why shouldn't I commit myself to it, trusting God to equip me with whatever gifts I need? No, I shouldn't push myself forward without consulting other believers—and yes, we must avoid trying to put square pegs into round holes. But when it needs to be done, why shouldn't Timothy take up the work of an evangelist (2 Tim 4:5)? Or why shouldn't Titus take the initiative in an important project (2 Cor 8:17)—or Onesiphorus go on helping Paul (2 Tim 1:16-18)?—or believers go out into the world for the Lord's sake (3 John 5-8)?

---

[17] Rom 12:6-8; 1 Cor 12:8-10, 28-30; Eph 4:11-12; 1 Pet 4:10-11.

Worth pondering ...

Nothing furthers this unity [that of the Spirit] more than the fact that different people are assigned different gifts of the Spirit, which are nothing other than ministries for building up that unity. If you offer your gifts to the church you will keep them as you ought and they will be a blessing to you—not just the gifts themselves but also the grace [of God who gave them]. But if you do not offer your gifts to the church and either neglect what has been given to you or abuse it for your own glory, profit or even to cause scandal to your neighbor, you will not be using it properly, and both the grace and the gift will be taken away from you by a God who is just.[18]

God employs a wonderful way to draw us to himself, which is by distributing his gifts in such a way to us that each one of us needs to be helped and succoured by his neighbours... each one of us must endeavour to make what God has given him available to the profit and advancement of his brethren. At the same time he must be content to borrow from other men and must allow himself to be helped and succoured at their hands ...[19]

[If] you have a grace or gift your fellow Christian does not have, use it in such a way that he is served by it. Do not be puffed up because of it, and do not despise him who does not have gifts of this kind. In this way you wash his feet as Christ has commanded.[20]

The distribution of the gifts of God is not human will, but at the will and pleasure of God who gives them as he pleases, to some more and to some less as he sees it expedient for his glory and our salvation. Therefore let none be despised because he has little, nor no one proud because he has much or more than another. Let everyone exercise and use their gifts given them, to the glory of God and the profit of others, and so be thankful to God the giver of all goodness, who gives his gifts not all to one person lest he should despise all others and abuse the gifts of God.[21]

---

[18] Johannes Bugenhagen in Gerald Bray (ed), Galatians, Ephesians, RCS: NT X (IVP Academic, 2011), 330.

[19] John Calvin, Sermons on the Epistle to the Ephesians (Banner of Truth, 1973 [1562]), 336.

[20] Martin Luther in Ewald Plass (ed), What Luther Says: An Anthology (Concordia, 1959), 3.1283.

[21] Lancelot Ridley in Gerald Bray (ed), Galatians, Ephesians, RCS: NT X (IVP Academic, 2011), 330..

3. Christian ministry is dependent on God's gifts

3.2. There are many different ministry gifts.

3.2.2. no one has all the gifts.

3.2.3. that is why we serve together: Christian ministry is collaborative. [22]

Hence all of the "co-" words in Paul, and all of the colleagues he names. This is also why local church leadership in the New Testament is a shared responsibility.[23]

Christian ministry belongs to all of God's people. Every believer is called to serve the Lord Jesus—and every believer is gifted by the Spirit for this purpose (1 Cor 12:7, 11). Because these gifts are very diverse, and because no one could ever have them all, it takes all of us working together to do what needs to be done for the church and by the church. So ministry is not what only some do: it is not one-way traffic, what the active members (the ministers or leaders) do to or for the passive members (the rest of the church).

The New Testament looks at our ministry from two main angles: it is what we do face-to-face and also what we do side-by-side. We are to do it for each other and also with each other. The first of these twin perspectives means that we must relate to each other in a way that reveals and increases our harmony. So ministry is to be exercised mutually: we are to serve one another in love (Gal 5:13). That is why the New Testament sets out a wide range of "one another" activities: many different ways in which we are responsible for each other and should be involved with each other.[24] This is the interactive aspect of ministry—but it also has a collaborative side. This second aspect concerns the side-by-side dimension of our life together: we must relate to each other in a way that

---

22 Rom 16:3, 9, 21; 1 Cor 3:5-10; 2 Cor 1:19; 8:23; Phil 1:4-5; 2:22, 25; 4:2-3; Col 1:7; 4:7; 1 Thess 3:2; Phm 1-2, 24.

23 Acts 11:25; 13:1; 14:23; 20:17, 28; 1 Cor 16:15-16; Phil 1:1; 1 Thess 5:12-13; 1 Tim 5:17.

24 John 13:34-35; 15:12; Rom 12:10, 16; 13:8; 14:13, 19; 15:5, 7, 14; 16:16; 1 Cor 12:25; Gal 5:13; 6:2; Eph 4:2, 32; 5:21; Phil 2:3; Col 3:9, 13; 1 Thess 3:12; 4:9, 18; 5:11, 15; 2 Thess 1:3; Heb 10:24; Jas 5:16; 1 Pet 1:22; 4:9; 5:5; 1 John 1:7; 3:11, 23; 4:7, 11-12; 2 John 5.

reveals and increases our solidarity. This is where we stand shoulder to shoulder as partners in God's work. Some of this will involve our teamwork within the body of Christ. Here our focus is discipleship, where we are aiming to grow believers in Christian maturity and also to equip them for effective service. We will also exercise this partnership facing outwards towards the world. Here our chief focus is evangelism, as we seek to reach the world for Christ by spreading the gospel as widely as possible.

This is such an important aspect of our new life as Christians, and was such a powerful reality in the early church, that the New Testament almost speaks a new language when talking about it. We see this in the way the apostles took over words and ideas from various backgrounds and used them in new ways. A good example is Paul's comparison of the church with the human body[25]—an image that in his world was used of the nation-state and even of the cosmos. One of the chief points he wants to make is that the church only grows as it should when every believer is actively contributing to its life (Eph 4:16; Col 2:19).

The New Testament not only uses words in new ways; it also uses new words. We find Paul using around twenty-five compound Greek words beginning with the prefix *syn-* ("with"), to speak about people who were involved in his ministry or about activities in which believers participate together. Some of these words seem to have been coined by him so that he had a way of talking about this togetherness in ministry.

The importance of serving together is highlighted by another feature of Paul's letters. This is the frequency with which refers to people who were involved in his mission and churches. It is remarkable how many individuals he names, given that he also makes general comments about such people without giving their names. The greatest concentration is found in Romans 16, where Paul names thirty-five different people, as well as referring to others whom he doesn't name. In his letters as a whole, we find nearly a hundred named individuals. At least one third of these are being acknowledged as having some role in his mission.

---

[25] Rom 12:4-5; 1 Cor 12:12-27; Eph 1:22-23; 4:4, 12, 15-16; 5:23, 29-30; Col 1:18, 24; 2:19; 3:15.

Also remarkable is the way he refers to these people. His status as Christ's apostle to the Gentiles and his consequent leadership of the Gentile mission did not lead him to speak of them as subordinates or underlings. Instead, his references to them often use the compound words we have already mentioned, indicating that he viewed them as partners in the great enterprise he led. In addition to "partner", he also uses such terms as "coworker", "fellow soldier", "fellow prisoner", "fellow slave", and the like.[26] Such evidence shows that Paul preferred to see these people as serving alongside him rather than as working under him. It is clear that he attached great importance to the fact that we are called to serve together.

Our collaboration in God's work takes place at various levels. One of these is the leadership of the local church, which the New Testament presents as something shared by a group of people. These came to be known as "seniors" ("elders") or "supervisors" ("overseers").[27] Their primary responsibility was teaching and shepherding the church.[28] Because of the many ways in which our society differs from theirs, we will not be able to reproduce the precise form that these roles took in the apostolic period. But what we can and must do is to ensure that leadership in our churches is a shared responsibility as it was in theirs.

Leadership solo-style is not good for the leader or for the led. Integrity can easily be eroded when there is no real accountability—and it is not difficult for the lone leader to find ways of avoiding scrutiny. This opens the door to sins such as pride, prayerlessness, manipulative abuses of power, the pretence involved in hiding behind a false ministry persona, and many others. So even where there is only one paid ministry-position in a church, it is very important to have other suitably-gifted people involved in leading the church alongside the paid worker.

Serving the Lord means serving his people and also serving with his people. That is because Christian ministry is both interactive and collaborative: we are to serve each other in harmony and to serve together

---

[26] Rom 16:3, 7, 9, 21; 2 Cor 8:23; Phil 1:7; 2:25; 4:3; Col 1:7; 4:7, 10, 11; Phm 1, 23, 24.

[27] For "seniors" (*presbuteroi*): see Acts 14:23; 20:17; 1 Tim 5:17; Tit 1:5; Jas 5:14; 1 Pet 5:1; for "supervisors" (*episkopoi*): see Acts 20:28; Phil 1:1; 1 Tim 3:2; Tit 1:7.

[28] Acts 20:28; Eph 4:11; 1 Tim 3:2; 5:17; Tit 1:9; 1 Pet 5:1-2.

in solidarity. So in some of our service we are all the same, while in some we are all different. The first is what we do as members of the family of God. This is where we express our love for each other as brothers and sisters, discharging the "one another" responsibilities we all share equally. Then there is what we do as members of the body of Christ. This is where we all contribute to the upward growth of the church and the outward reach of the gospel, to the mission of the church as well as its maturity. But because we are gifted differently, our contributions in the work of evangelism or of edification will vary. Being servants binds us together in our fellowship and in our partnership.

Worth pondering ...

[Because] the Lord does not give all these gifts and skills just to one, two, or three, churches have always had a good number of elders, and these not all the same in what they do and what they are... there is so much involved in the true care of souls that even those who are most skilled in this ministry, if they are alone or few in number, will not achieve very much; because all skill and ability comes from God, who desires to carry out this his work in his church by means of many and not by means of few... None of his members must be idle, and there must be the highest degree of unity and order among them, each one must depend on and be depended on by the other ...[29]

We must remember ... that the preacher (or pastor) is also fundamentally one of the elders of his congregation. This means that many decisions involving the church yet not requiring the attention of all the members should fall not to the pastor alone but to the elders as a whole. While this is sometimes cumbersome, it has the immense benefits of rounding out the pastor's gifts, making up for some of his deficiencies, supplementing his judgment, and creating congregational support for decisions, leaving leaders less exposed to unjust criticism. It also makes leadership more rooted and permanent and allows for more mature continuity.[30]

Every church should have elders because pastors need help and accountability... Without help from properly qualified and gifted men who can share in this important work, a lone pastor will be crushed by the weight of ministry. God's design is that a group of leaders share this burden together. This ... provides the church balance by offering a variety of perspectives and gifts... In addition, elders provide needed accountability... Many pastors have too much authority and too little accountability ... Biblical accountability protects the character and witness of elders and fosters maturity and godliness among them as they challenge each other toward love and good deeds.[31]

---

[29] Martin Bucer, Concerning the True Care of Souls (Banner of Truth, 2009 [1538]), 55, 58.

[30] Mark Dever, Nine Marks of a Healthy Church, new expanded edition (Crossway, 2004), 230f.

[31] Benjamin L. Merkle, Why Elders? A Biblical and Practical Guide for Church Members (Kregel, 2009), 60.

[No] one person has the sufficient gifting, or energy, or insight, or perspective, to fulfill all that is needed in the governing and teaching of a local church. Not only do many hands often make light work, many hands often make better and more complete work... No one is adequate in himself, but together a plurality of elders can provide collectively what is lacking from any one person individually.[32]

---

[32] Bruce A. Ware in Benjamin L. Merkle & Thomas R. Schreiner (eds), *Shepherding God's Flock: Biblical Leadership in the New Testament and Beyond* (Kregel, 2014), 295.

3. Christian ministry is dependent on God's gifts

3.3. There are two main types of service.

3.3.1. some ministries are more basic than others.

3.3.2. hence the "some for all" pattern of ministry.

Christian ministry belongs to all of God's people. All of us have been called to serve the Lord Jesus, and the Holy Spirit has equipped each one of us to do so. Because the body only grows and functions as it should when all of its different parts are working in unison, in the body of Christ we are meant to serve together as partners.

It is therefore surprising to discover what Peter tells us about ministry. He says that we are stewards of God's richly diverse grace, because each of us has received a gift that equips us to serve others (1 Pet 4:10). He then mentions those who speak and those who serve, indicating how we should do both of these things (1 Pet 4:11). What can he mean by making this distinction? How can serving be what only some of us do when he has just said that we are all supposed to serve? And shouldn't speaking God's words be counted as a way of serving? What is this passage trying to tell us?[33]

Peter says what he says about our service because of what is true of our salvation. Our new life begins with new birth—and this work of God comes about only through the word of God (1 Pet 1:23-25). The story of our lives as Christians begins with the gospel, the word of truth (1 Pet 1:12, 22). But this is not a launch-pad we leave further and further behind the longer we go on as Christians; it is the foundation on which the whole of the Christian life rests. If we are to continue as believers, we must stand firm both in the faith and in the grace of God (1 Pet 5:9, 12). We can only do this by holding fast to the gospel, which is the faith by which we live and also the message which teaches us about God's grace. If God's gospel word is our point-of-entry into his great salvation and also the foundation for our lives as believers, then there is one ministry that is more fundamental than all the others: the ministry of announcing and teaching

---

[33] Note how Paul makes a similar distinction between serving and teaching (Rom 12:7).

God's word. That is why Peter distinguishes speaking from every other kind of serving (1 Pet 4:11).

The point that Peter makes very briefly is made at greater length by Paul in Ephesians 4:7-13. Once again, the starting-point is the grace that gifts each one of us (Eph 4:7), and the subject is the serving that all of God's people are to do (Eph 4:12). And once again, we find an unexpected distinction being made. While ministry is what belongs to all believers, there are some who receive special mention (Eph 4:11). Two important points are made about these people. Their role is to equip everyone else for service (Eph 4:12), and the risen, reigning Jesus has given them to his church for this purpose (Eph 4:8-12). So Christian ministry depends on gifts of two different kinds: the grace given to each of us (Eph 4:7) and also the people given to all of us (Eph 4:11). This is the crucial "some for all" pattern that the Lord has embedded in the life of his church: the ministry of some undergirds and enables the ministry of all.

How do the four groups Paul mentions do this equipping? The answer is not hard to find when we consider what they have in common. Those who are apostles or prophets or evangelists or pastor-teachers all have a ministry of God's word. This is what we all need—and need all the time—if we are to work with God and for him. Only when we are being instructed by God's word will we know what goals and methods our ministries should have. And only when we are being ruled and changed by God's word will we do God's work in God's way. Those who were, like Paul, both apostles and prophets had a role that was unique and foundational (Eph 2:20; 3:2-7). They planted the seed of the word in God's field; they laid the foundation of the gospel for God's building (1 Cor 3:5-6, 9-11). They now convey God's word to us in the New Testament Scriptures. Those who are evangelists and pastor-teachers have an ongoing role: from the apostles' time onwards, they have been planting and shepherding churches by proclaiming and teaching the word of God.

It is important not to misunderstand the distinction Paul is making here. He does not mean that evangelists and pastor-teachers are exempt from works of service! Their ministry of the word is the primary way in which they serve the Lord and his people—and this will be done in the context of the mutual care and service by which we all express love for each other (Gal 5:13) and by which we together grow to maturity (Eph 4:11-

13, 16). So pastor-teachers do not sit on the sidelines while the rest of us are serving. Rather, they are meant to be like the playing coach of a sporting team. This is someone who is a member of the team like all the rest, and so plays each game beside them. Yet he or she is distinguished from all the others by having the responsibility for training the team in order to get the best out of them. And in order to ensure that this training is done as well as possible, the sporting club involved may pay the playing-coach so that this role is also his/her job—so while the other members of the team are busy in the workplace, he or she can concentrate on planning and running the team's training-regime.

So it is with pastor-teachers. First and foremost, they are members of Christ's body, engaged with their fellow-believers in the service that grows their church (Eph 4:16)—but they also have the responsibility of training and equipping other believers for this vital work. They will do this by praying for them and with them, by teaching them God's word, by encouraging and caring for them, by inviting them to work alongside them in particular tasks or ministries, and so on. What they do is not different in kind from what we all should be doing—but it is different in its focus or intensity, because it is their primary occupation.

It is important to recognise that the only kind of pastor the New Testament knows is the pastor-teacher. This alerts us to the most crucial feature of Christian shepherding: at its heart will be the teaching of God's word (Mark 6:34). The principal way in which pastors lead and care for the Good Shepherd's sheep is to bring God's word to them and to bring them to God's word. Paul makes this very clear in his address to the elders of the church in Ephesus (Acts 20:17-35). He urges them to keep watch over all the flock as shepherds of God's church (20:28)—which raises the question of how he expects them to do this. The answer is obvious as soon as we think about what his speech is doing. He reminds them in some detail of the ministry he exercised among them, emphasizing the fact that he concentrated on proclaiming and teaching and applying God's word (verses 20-21, 24, 25, 27, 31). This reminder is obviously meant as a call for them to model their ministry on his: to feed and guard God's flock with his word.

This is not something that only church leaders are meant to do, however. The work of shepherding by teaching God's word should normally be happening at a number of different levels within the life of every church.[34] This should be what all of its members do with and for each other. Note how Paul urges the Colossians to keep the gospel at the centre of their fellowship by teaching and admonishing one another— which is exactly what he does in his ministry as Christ's apostle (Col 1:28; 3:16). Likewise, the Thessalonians are to encourage each other with Paul's words and to be involved in what we would call "pastoral care" (1 Thess 4:18; 5:11, 14-15). Since these believers mostly met as house-churches, this mutual teaching and exhorting is bound to have happened in their regular meetings. Probably the nearest equivalent for most of us is the home-group which meets regularly to study the Bible, to pray, and to support and encourage each other—and leading such a group gives me a special responsibility for shepherding the members.

There are also other ways in which this mutual, face-to-face engagement with God's word should be happening. Married men will do this with their wife and children; each of us could do it for a few others with whom we meet individually on a regular basis; some will do it as the pastor-teacher of the whole church—and some will do it at several or even all of these levels. So the fact that a pastor and/or elders are engaged in shepherding the church does not mean that its members are expected to be passive, sheep who do no shepherding. If God's word is to do its essential work in our lives and in our church, each of us can and should make sure that it stays at the centre of all that we do.

The work of God is grounded in the word of God—so the ministry of God's word must always be at the heart of our lives and ministries as God's people, in our mutual interaction and also in the labours of the shepherds of God's flock. They must give themselves to this "ministry of the word" so that we are all equipped for the service that grows and builds God's church.

---

34   Rom 12:7; 15:14; Gal 6:6; Eph 4:14-15, 29; Col 3:16; 4:6; Tit 2:3-5; Heb 5:12; 10:23-25.

Worth pondering ...

[All] strengthening of the weak and ailing sheep depends on the word of God being faithfully set forth to them, and them being led to listen to it gladly... So this is how the weak and ailing sheep of Christ are to be strengthened and comforted, and this is to be done by all Christians. For since Christ lives in all his members, he will also exercise this pastoral work of his in all.[35]

Inasmuch as the office of preaching the gospel is the greatest of all and certainly is apostolic, it becomes the foundation of all other functions, which are built upon it...For since the church owes its birth to the Word, is nourished, aided and strengthened by it, it is obvious that it cannot be without the Word. If it is without the Word it ceases to be a church.[36]

The first great duty of the ministry...is the dispensation of the doctrine of the gospel unto [the church], for its edification. As this is the duty of the church to attend unto...so it is the principal work of the ministry, the foundation of all other duties...for this is the principal means appointed by Christ for the edification of his church, that whereby spiritual life is begotten and preserved. Where this work is neglected or carelessly attended unto, there the whole work of the ministry is despised.[37]

The Lord Jesus himself is the Good Shepherd who laid down his life for the sheep, the Great Shepherd who is brought again from the dead, and the Chief Shepherd under whom he has appointed shepherds to watch for the souls of men. He will have those of us whom he calls to his service to shepherdize those who are converted: leading, protecting, feeding, comforting, and succouring them. He will call us to account if we neglect this charge...[38]

All believers are called to salvation, service, sacrifice, and simplicity...Every member of the household of faith is in some way a pastor, a missionary, a theologian, and a servant leader.[39]

---

[35] Martin Bucer, Concerning the True Care of Souls (Banner of Truth, 2009 [1538]), 167, 171.
[36] Martin Luther, Works (Concordia, 1958 [1523]), 40.36, 37.
[37] John Owen, Works (Banner of Truth, 1967 [1677]), 4.508f.
[38] C.H. Spurgeon, The Metropolitan Tabernacle Pulpit (Pilgrim, 1973 [1882]), 28.566.
[39] Douglas D. Webster, Living in Tension: A Theology of Ministry, Volume 1. The Nature of Ministry: Faithfulness from the Beginning (Cascade, 2012), xi-xii.

NOTE:

The discussion above has interpreted Ephesians 4:11-12 in two ways that some interpreters past and present disagree with. The first turns on the number of commas your translation of the Bible uses! Some commentators argue that the right way of understanding what Paul says is what we find in the King James Bible: "he gave some ... for the perfecting of the saints, for the work of the ministry, for the edifying of the body of Christ." This means that the four groups specified in verse 11 have been given to serve in three ways: to perfect the saints, to do the work of ministry, and to build up the body of Christ. So the work of ministry Paul is referring to belongs only to them and not to all of us. More recent translations omit the first comma, so that the sentence now reads (in the NASB): "He gave some...for the equipping of the saints for the work of service, to the building up of the body of Christ..." Here, the work of ministry belongs to all of God's people, and the role of those the Lord has given to his church is to equip them to do it. That this is more likely to be what Paul means is demonstrated by what he says in verse 16. This makes it clear that the growth and upbuilding of the body comes about through the active contribution of each one of its many parts. Since the building up of the body is not the work of just a few, it is difficult to believe that in verse 12 Paul would intend to limit "the work of serving" just to the four groups in verse 11.

The second area of disagreement is whether verse 11 is speaking of five groups or four. Are the nouns "pastor" and "teacher" referring to two distinct groups or just one, with the two nouns indicating complementary aspects of their role? The underlying issues are fairly technical, so it is not easy to do justice to them here—but as my discussion of the passage shows, I think that Paul is speaking about "pastor-teachers". Apart from the technical reasons for this conclusion, the New Testament makes it fairly clear that there is no true shepherding that does not have teaching and applying God's word at its heart – as we see in the ministry of the good shepherd (Mark 6:34; 10:1).

Part 4: THE FOCUS OF CHRISTIAN MINISTRY

4. Christian ministry is focused ...

4.1. on God's Son.

He is our message.[1] Our ministries are from him,[2] and also for him.[3]

What we have learned about Christian ministry to this point shows that it has many dimensions and needs to be viewed from many angles. This raises an important question: Is there something that gives it cohesion, a centre to which everything is connected, a hub that binds all the spokes together? We are not asking whether we can find something to put in the centre, for we are not meant to be in charge here. Since it is God's work we are involved in, the question is rather whether the Bible gives it such a centre. In the Bible, is there something that binds all the different elements of Christian ministry together? Where should we be focusing as we carry out our ministries? Is there a centre without which our work is not properly Christian? We discover the answer to these questions in what the Bible tells us about the way God is doing his work.

We see this integrating centre in the purpose of the Father, which is that all should give the highest honour to the Son (John 5:22-23; Phil 2:9-11). We see it in the work of the Spirit, all of which is aimed at glorifying the Son (John 16:14). We see it in the Scriptures, which are all about the Lord Jesus.[4] We see it in the gospel, which is the gospel of Christ or the word of Christ.[5] Its subject is the worth of Christ: it is "the gospel of the glory of Christ" (2 Cor 4:4, NASB).[6] It presents him as the Father's unique Son, the Lord of all, the Saviour of the world. So the gospel is the word of Christ about the worth of Christ. The gospel also centres on what he has done for us: it is the word of Christ about the work of Christ. It is

---

[1] Acts 8:5; 9:20; 11:19-20; 1 Cor 1:22-24; 2:2; 3:11; 2 Cor 4:5; Eph 3:8; Phil 1:15-18; Col 1:28; Heb 13:7-8.
[2] Eph 4:7, 11-13; Col 4:17; 1 Tim 1:12.
[3] Acts 5:41; Rom 1:5; Col 3:17; 3 John 7.
[4] Luke 24:25-27, 44; John 5:39, 46; Rom 1:1-4.
[5] Rom 1:9; 10:17, NASB; 15:19; 1 Cor 9:12; 2 Cor 2:12; 9:13; 10:14; Gal 1:7; Phil 1:27; Col 3:16, NASB; 2 Thess 1:8.
[6] Rom 1:1-4, 9; Eph 3:7-8; 2 Tim 2:8.

"the message of the cross" because it concerns Christ crucified.[7] It also proclaims his resurrection from the dead and exaltation to heavenly rule as Lord of all.[8] In all of this it is the gospel of salvation (Eph 1:13), because it announces the comprehensive salvation that he has won for us. This stems from the complete sufficiency of his saving work, which in its turn is grounded in the absolute supremacy of his person. No one is greater or higher than him—and there is no one who could be. As a result, what his work has won for us could not be greater or richer in any way. The Bible makes it very clear that everything in God's word and work focuses on his Son. If we are to do God's work in God's way, the Lord Jesus himself must therefore be the focus and centre of our ministries.

So he is our message: "we proclaim him" (Col 1:28, NASB). We have nothing to offer the world except the Lord Jesus—and he is also what the church needs all the time. This is what distinguishes the gospel from an ideology. Christian preaching and teaching is more than setting out theological ideas we want our hearers to embrace. The truth we declare is the vehicle by which the Lord himself comes to us. Yes, people must receive and hold fast to the truth—but this means much more than committing to a particular doctrinal framework or worldview. By proclaiming the word of truth, we are inviting the world to meet and know a glorious Person. To proclaim the gospel is to proclaim Christ: it is the word of Christ, and its subject is the glory of Christ.[9] So the right response when people hear the gospel is not only to believe it but also to believe in him.[10] The only way we come to know him and to be united with him is to believe in him—and it is only the apostolic message that enables us to do this.[11]

This two-in-one response to the Lord and the word forms the core of the Christian life, which is always grounded both "in him" and "in the

---

7   1 Cor 1:17-18, 23; 15:1-3; Gal 3:1-2.

8   Acts 2:32-36; Rom 1:1-4; 1 Cor 15:1-5, 12, 15,20-26; Eph 1:20-23; Phil 2:9-11; 1 Thess 1:9- 10; 2 Tim 2:8; 1 Pet 3:21-22; Rev 1:5, 18.

9   Acts 8:4-5, 25; 13:49; 16:31-32; 19:20; 2 Cor 4:2-5; Eph 3:7-8; Phil 1:12-18; Col 3:16, NASB.

10   Believing the gospel: see Mark 1:15; Acts 17:11-12; 1 Cor 1:21; 15:11; Gal 3:2, 5; 2 Thess 1:10; 1 Pet 3:1. Believing in the Lord through the gospel: see Acts 16:14-15; Eph 1:13-15; Col 1:3-7; 1 Thess 1:4-8; 1 Pet 1:8-9, 12.

11   John 17:3, 20-21, 25-26; Acts 11:20-21; 15:7-11; 16:14-15,30-34; Rom 15:20; 2 Cor 2:12, 14; Gal 3:22, 26; 4:3-9; Col 1:3-7; 2:5-7; 2 Thess 1:8; 1 John 1:1-3; 2:12-14; 4:6-16.

faith". To receive him, we must be taught the faith (Col 2:6-7). And we remain in him only as the gospel remains in us (1 John 2:24). If we let go of the gospel, we lose hold of him.[12] And where people are denying him, we must contend for the faith (Jude 3-4). So the focus of the gospel is not a *what*, a truth or an idea, but a *who*, our Lord and Saviour Jesus Christ. It declares his worth and his work, and directs us to him as the one we should trust and obey. It brings him to us and it is meant to take us to him.

He is not only the content of our message; he is also the source and the goal of our ministries. All of Christian ministry is derived from his grace and should be aimed at his glory. In the New Testament, ministry itself is a gift of his grace. It is given to us, not generated by us. We receive it from him: it comes to us, not from us. This is not only true of Paul; it is true of all who serve.[13] Ministry is also made possible by his grace-gifts: we are able to serve because he both equips and empowers us to do so.[14] So all ministry comes from the Lord—and all of it is meant to be for him.

The overriding goal of our ministry should be to exalt him. We ought to serve in such a way that as many people as possible will give him the love and loyalty that is his by right, responding from the heart to his worth and work as our Lord and Saviour. So nothing about our ministries is meant to revolve around us; it should be all about him. We could not find a better ministry-motto than that of John the Baptizer: "He must become greater; I must become less" (John 3:30).

Nothing in Christian service is more important than this! In life and ministry, the Lord Jesus Christ must be our unwavering focus. We are to find our hope and joy, our security and significance, in him and his gospel, not in ourselves and our ministries. We must be clear that there is only one thing of surpassing worth—and this is not what we are or do, but knowing Christ Jesus as Lord (Phil 3:8). He should be our message and our model, our foundation and our motivation, our focus and our treasure. This gives us a fundamental question we should ask ourselves

---

12 2 Cor 11:2-4; Gal 1:6; 5:4; 2 John 9.

13 Acts 20:24, 28; Rom 15:15-16; 1 Cor 3:5; 15:9-10; 2 Cor 4:1; 5:18; 10:8, 13; Gal 1:15- 16; 2:7; Eph 3:2, 7-8; Col 1:25; 4:17; 1 Thess 2:4; 1 Tim 1:12; 4:14-16; 6:20; 2 Tim 1:6; Tit 1:3.

14 1 Cor 12:4-11, 31; 14:1, 12; Eph 4:7, 11-13; Phil 4:13; Col 1:29; 1 Tim 1:12; 2 Tim 4:17; 1 Pet 4:10-11.

every day: In my life and ministry, is the Lord Jesus where he should be and what he should be?

Worth pondering ...

Between Christ and the gospel there exists an unbreakable bond...So whenever we hear God's word preached, let us look to our Lord Jesus Christ: he is the goal at which we aim. We can be sure that in him we have all that belongs to the hope of our salvation. For the rest, when men speak to us of Jesus Christ, let us not picture him as some sort of phantom...but let us come to the gospel where he may be known, where we learn why God his Father sent him to us, the blessing he has brought and his ministry to us. Since the gospel clearly shows us these things, we may safely regard it as a true mirror in which we behold our God in the image of the Lord Jesus Christ...[15]

There is one article and one basic principle in theology, and he who does not hold to this article and this basic truth, to wit, true faith and trust in Christ, is no theologian. All the other articles flow into and out of this one, and without it the others are nothing. The devil has tried from the beginning to nullify this article and to establish his own wisdom in its place. The disturbed, the afflicted, the troubled, and the tempted relish this article; they are the ones who understand the Gospel.[16]

[Preach] CHRIST, always and evermore. He is the whole gospel. His person, offices, and work must be our one great, all-comprehending theme.[17]

Jesus Christ alone is the hope, treasure, joy, and purpose of pastoral ministry. Not church growth, not church planting, not church success, not church business...Let everything be a means to this end: the treasuring of Christ and the enjoying of his glory. The pastor is not the missional conqueror—Jesus is. The pastor is not the chief shepherd—Jesus is. The pastor is not the lord of the kingdom—Jesus is.[18]

---

15 John Calvin, Sermons on Titus (Banner of Truth, 2015 [1561]), 28 [on 1:1-4].
16 Martin Luther in Ewald Plass (ed), What Luther Says: An Anthology (Concordia, 1959), 3.1357.
17 C.H. Spurgeon, Lectures to My Students (Hendrickson, 2010 [1875]), 82.
18 Jared C. Wilson, The Pastor's Justification: Applying the Work of Christ to Your Life and Ministry (Crossway, 2013), 155.

4. Christian ministry is focused ...

4.2. on God's work.

> This is the work of mission, winning the world.[19] It is also the work of maturity, growing the church.[20] In all of this is the work of majesty, in which God displays his glory.[21]

Out of his great grace, God gives us a place in his work, conferring upon us the great dignity of being his co-workers. But what is that work? What does God want us to do with him? The Bible gives us many ways of answering this important question. Perhaps the most fundamental answer, capable of including all the others, lies in the great word "salvation". This is why Mary's son was called "Jesus" (Matt 1:21). This is why he came into the world.[22] This is why he shares God's title of Saviour.[23] In a lost world that is under judgment, God is at work bringing in his great salvation. This saving work has two principal dimensions, which we can call mission and maturity.

The work of mission is a wide work. This is where God works out his purpose to bring his salvation to the ends of the earth.[24] He is gathering into his church people from every part of the world, from every human society, so that at the End those who have been saved will form a vast assembly whose members come "from every nation, tribe, people and language" (Rev 7:9). But there is only one doorway into salvation, only one name that can save us (John 10:9; Acts 4:12). So no one can become a member of that great assembly without knowing that salvation belongs to God and to the Lamb (Rev 7:10). And it is the gospel of salvation (Eph

---

[19] Isa 45:20-22; Matt 24:14; 28:18-20; Luke 24:46-47; John 3:17; 4:42; 12:32; 17:14-18; Acts 1:8; Rom 1:5; 16:26; 2 Cor 5:18-20; 1 John 4:14.

[20] 1 Cor 3:9-15; Eph 2:19-22; 4:11-16; Col 2:19; 1 Thess 3:12-13; 4:9; 5:23-24.

[21] Psa 96:2-9; 145:3-21; Isa 12:2-5; 66:18-19; Ezek 20:5-22, 30-44; 36:22-28; Hab 2:14; Eph 1:12-14; 3:10-11, 20-21; 1 Tim 1:15-17; Rev 7:9-12.

[22] Luke 19:10; John 3:17; 4:42; 12:47; 1 Tim 1:15; 2 Tim 1:9-10; Heb 5:7-9; 9:26-28; 1 John 4:9-10, 14.

[23] Luke 1:47; 2:11; John 4:42; Acts 5:31; 13:23; Phil 3:20; 1 Tim 1:1; 2:3; 4:10; 2 Tim 1:10; Tit 1:3, 4; 2:10, 13; 3:4, 6; 1 John 4:14; Jude 25.

[24] Psa 65:2-5; 74:12; 96:1-3; 98:1-4; Isa 25:6-9; 45:20-21; 49:6; 52:7-10.

1:13) that gives us that knowledge. That is why we have been sent to plant the gospel in the life of every people and nation.[25]

If the gospel is to take root and keep growing in each people-group, it must be communicated in culturally-sensitive ways, the Bible must be translated, and evangelists and pastor-teachers must be trained. This missionary task of the church remains in force until the Lord comes. It must always have high priority: in each generation, we must send gifted people into this vital work. But this does not mean that we send only a few; we must send as many as possible. The Lord does his work with the army of the willing; he is not reliant on a few super-stars (1 Cor 1:26-29).

The work of maturity is a deep work. This is where God grows his church to its full stature and brings it to wholeness and perfection in Christ. In this way, he completes his saving purpose, bringing in his full and final salvation. He takes us to this glorious destiny by doing his saving work in us, growing us and changing us: we are being saved now so that we will be saved entirely then.[26] This process has two sides: as God is growing us, we are to keep growing up in our salvation (1 Pet 2:2). Because he is working his saving purpose in us, we are to work out our salvation (Phil 2:12-13). The gospel is the key here too. God called us into his salvation through the gospel—and we remain inside that salvation by holding firmly to the gospel.[27] If we are to grow up in our salvation, we need "the pure milk of the word" (1 Pet 2:2, NASB). It is only when the gospel keeps bearing fruit and growing in our lives that we bear fruit and grow in our knowledge of God (Col 1:6, 10). For us to grow to maturity in Christ we need the ongoing ministry of the gospel, where Jesus Christ is proclaimed and we are admonished and taught with all wisdom (Col 1:28). In order to be built up in him, we need to be strengthened in the faith (Col 2:7), the gospel that was taught to us (Col 1:6-7). As the gospel, the word of God's grace, does its work we will be built up and brought into our heavenly inheritance (Acts 20:32).

So the foundation on which God's saving work in us rests is the gospel: he changes us and grows us by working his word more and more

---

[25] Matt 28:18-20; Luke 24:46-47; Acts 1:8.
[26] Rom 5:9-10; 1 Cor 1:18; 2 Cor 2:15; 1 Thess 5:8-9; 2 Tim 2:10; Heb 1:14; 7:25; 9:28; 1 Pet 1:3-5.
[27] 1 Cor 15:1-2; 2 Thess 2:13-15.

deeply into our lives. There are many ways by which he does this, but one of the most central is the ministry of the pastor-teacher. So in every generation, we must send gifted people into this work too. But again, this is not reserved for a handful of super-stars. It needs a great many ordinary recruits: believers of good character who are able to teach the word of God (Tit 1:6-9), and who are willing to work hard for the sake of Jesus and the gospel.

In this wide and deep saving work, God is displaying his unique and unsurpassable majesty as Lord and Saviour. All the glory of his greatness and goodness is seen in his saving work. Through his wide work of mission, the world is being filled with the knowledge of God's glory (Hab 2:14); through his deep work of maturity, his glory is reflected in the church (Eph 3:21). He does all of this out of his grace: his never merited, never limited love for hostile rebels.[28] But there is something even more fundamental and important than this.

God does all of his saving work for the sake of his name: to reveal his matchless glory as God.[29] This should lead us to glory in his holy name (Psa 105:3): the glory he is showing us is meant to be echoed by the glory we are giving him. This will be embodied in our worship and our witness: we will glorify God by our praise and adoration, and by the witness of our gospel proclamation and godly living.[30]

Our participation in God's work of mission and maturity thus has a higher goal than bringing people into his salvation and growing them up in that salvation. Our overriding aim and our greatest longing in all of this must be to give as many people as possible as many reasons as possible to join us in adoring our glorious Saviour throughout the endless ages to come (Rev 5:13; 7:9-10).

---

[28] Neh 9:16-18, 29-31; Psa 103:8-12; 116:1-7; Isa 63:7-9; Acts 15:11; Rom 5:8-10; Eph 1:3-8; 2:4-9; 2 Tim 1:9-10; Tit 2:11-14; 3:4-7; 1 John 4:9-10.

[29] 1 Sam 12:22-24; Psa 25:11; 31:1-3; 79:9; 106:6-8; 109:21-27; Isa 43:25; 48:9-11; Jer 14:7-9, 20-22; Ezek 20:8-9, 13-14, 21-22, 44; Dan 9:17-19; Rom 1:5; Eph 1:6, 12, 14; 1 John 2:12.

[30] Matt 5:16; Rom 1:5; 11:33-36; 15:6, 9; 1 Cor 10:31-33; 2 Cor 4:15; Phil 1:9-11, 20-26; 2 Thess 1:11-12; 1 Tim 1:17; Heb 13:20-21; 1 Pet 2:12; 2 Pet 3:18; 3 John 5-8; Jude 25; Rev 1:5-6.

All that we do in Christian ministry must have a double focus: we must always be aiming both wide and deep, seeking to reach the world for Christ and to grow the church in Christ. Authentic Christian service will always give the highest priority to both of these dimensions of God's saving work. And it will do so to glorify the God who reveals his glory supremely in his Son and in the wide and deep work of the gospel.

This leaves me with a question I should ask myself often: can I honestly say that this is what motivates and shapes my ministry? Does the glory of God matter to me as much as it should? If not, why not? What am I not doing—and can start doing now—that would ensure that God is and remains supreme every day and in every part of my life and work?

Worth pondering ...

[If] God had simply proclaimed our pardon by declaring that he had decided to receive us in mercy, despite our unworthiness, that would have been a great thing. Even then, we would never have been able to utter sufficient praise for such grace. But God has given us his own Son as a token of his love. Indeed, he has given us himself through his Son, and declared himself to be our Father. This so far outshines pardon alone that even if we employed all our faculties to worship and adore, we could never perfectly praise him for such mercy.[31]

Servant-leaders are not visionaries who devise a brilliant plan, then by dint of personal charisma draw others to fulfill those ambitions. Rather they are faithful stewards of the divine mandate—to fish and to feed, to evangelize and to teach, to pioneer and to pastor. Biblical leadership maintains a laser-like concentration on God's clearly stated agenda, that is, the evangelization of the lost, the edification of the saved, and the establishment of vital churches.[32]

[The] work God is doing in the world now...between the first and second comings of Christ, is to gather people into his kingdom through the prayerful proclamation of the gospel...Simply by virtue of being a disciple of Jesus and filled with the Holy Spirit of the new covenant, all Christians have the privilege, joy and responsibility of being involved in the work God is doing ... and the fundamental way we do this is by speaking the truth of God to other people in dependence on the Holy Spirit.[33]

[The] love of God and the gospel of God are radically God-centered. God loves us by giving us himself to enjoy... Most people know that the greatest experiences of joy in this life—the ones that come closest to being pictures of perfect joy in heaven—are not experiences of self-affirmation, but of self-forgetfulness in the presence of something majestic...Seeing the glory of God in Christ is the highest gift and the greatest pleasure we are capable of. Giving us this is what love is.[34]

---

[31] John Calvin, Sermons on Galatians (Banner of Truth, 1997 [1563]), 24.
[32] Don N. Howell, Jr., Servants of the Servant: A Biblical Theology of Leadership (Wipf & Stock, 2003), 301.
[33] Colin Marshall & Tony Payne, The Trellis and the Vine: The Ministry Mind-Shift that Changes Everything (Matthias, 2009), 41, 49.
[34] John Piper, God is the Gospel: Meditations on God's Love as the Gift of Himself (Crossway, 2005), 148, 151, 154.

4. Christian ministry is focused ...

4.3. on some essential commitments.

The first and most important is prayer.[35]

Of all the commitments we should make in our ministries, this is the most essential! It is here that we determine whether the work we are doing really is God's work—or whether it is a series of projects we do for him but without him.

We see its importance in the central place prayer had in the ministry of Jesus. The Gospels not only record some of his prayers,[36] but also indicate that he frequently spent time in prayer.[37] There was undoubtedly a direct connection between his faithfulness in prayer and his undeviating loyalty to his Father's will. Prayer also had an important place in his teaching: Jesus made it clear that his disciples should be prayerful people.[38]

The importance of prayer is also seen in the example of the twelve apostles. While waiting for the promised gift of the Spirit, they continued in prayer (Acts 1:12-15). So it is not surprising that when the Spirit came, the new Christian community that emerged was devoted to prayer (Acts 2:42; 12:5). The apostles continued to set an example here (3:1; 6:6). When threatened with severe sanctions by the Jewish leadership, they prayed for God's help (Acts 4:23-30). When faced with the problem about food distribution, they made it clear that they must give priority to prayer along with their ministry of the word (Acts 6:4). Is it any wonder that "the word of God spread" (Acts 6:7)? In keeping with the example they set, in their letters the apostles encourage their readers to be people of prayer.[39]

---

35 Acts 4:23-31; 6:4; 10:9; 12:5; 13:3; 14:23; 16:25; 20:36; 21:5; 22:17; 28:8; Rom 1:8- 10; 12:12; 15:30-32; 1 Cor 1:4; 2 Cor 1:11; Eph 1:15-20; 3:14-19; 6:18-20; Phil 1:3-6, 9-11, 19; 4:6; Col 1:3-4, 9-12; 4:2-4, 12; 1 Thess 1:2-3; 2:13; 3:10; 2 Thess 1:11-12; 2 Tim 1:3; Phm 4-6.
36 Matt 11:25-26; 26:39, 42; Luke 23:34, 46; John 11:41-42; 12:28; 17:1-26.
37 Mark 1:35; 6:41, 46; Luke 3:21; 5:16; 6:12; 9:18, 28-29; 11:1; 22:32.
38 Matt 5:44; 6:5-15; 7:7-11; 18:19; Mark 11:24-25; Luke 11:1-13; 18:1-8; 21:36; 22:40, 46; John 14:13-14; 15:7, 16; 16:23-24, 26.
39 Jas 1:5-6; 4:2-3; 5:13-18; 1 Pet 3:7; 4:7; 1 John 3:21-22; 5:14-16.

The example and teaching of Paul provide more indications of the importance of prayer. Every day, he felt the pressure of his concern for the churches (2 Cor 11:28)—a concern that led him to pray for them regularly.[40] This example was followed by his co-workers (Col 4:12). Paul also taught his churches that they should be prayerful, and often asked them to pray for him.[41] One obvious reason why his letters report what he prayed for his readers was that this would teach them how they could pray, both thanking God for the work of grace he had done in their lives and asking him to keep taking it further and deeper.

There is thus no doubt that we should be praying people. The chief reason for this is that we are God's dearly loved children. The saving work done for us by the Lord Jesus has given us free and open access to our heavenly Father.[42] So for us his throne is a throne of grace, where we can go with confidence to ask for mercy and help.[43] And this is what we need all the time—so a clear sense of our own weakness and failings on the one hand and of the Lord's all-sufficiency on the other should keep us at prayer.[44] Not that we will come to him only to ask: he is so kind and generous, that we always have much to thank him for and much to praise him about. So we have many reasons for turning to him very often.

Our involvement in Christian ministry gives us an extra incentive to be prayerful. That is because everything we do for God is meant to be done with him: we should rely consciously and constantly on the Holy Spirit. What makes this essential is the fact that we are incapable of doing the work of the Lord: "apart from me you can do nothing" (John 15:5). As we were reminded in discussing 2.1.2 above, unbelievers are dead (Eph 2:1; Col 2:13)—and we cannot give them life; blind (2 Cor 4:4)—and we cannot make them see; lost (Luke 19:10)—and we cannot bring them home. We cannot change people and make them fit to be with God forever in his kingdom. Unless God is at work with us and through us,

---

[40] Rom 1:8-10; 1 Cor 1:4; Eph 1:15-20; 3:14-19; Phil 1:3-11; Col 1:3-4, 9-12; 1 Thess 1:2-3; 2:13; 3:10-13; 2 Thess 1:3, 11-12.

[41] Rom 12:12; 15:30-32; Eph 6:18-20; Phil 4:6; Col 4:2-4; 1 Thess 5:17, 25; 2 Thess 3:1-2; 1 Tim 2:1-8.

[42] Rom 5:1-2; Eph 2:13, 18; Heb 7:19, 25.

[43] Eph 3:12; Heb 4:16; 10:19-22; 1 John 5:14-15.

[44] Mark 14:38; Luke 22:31-34; 2 Cor 1:8-11; 2:16; 3:4-6; 12:8-9.

even our best efforts will end up being completely futile and fruitless. So everything we do for him must be undergirded with prayer.

We will often be reminded of this, no matter what ministry we are involved in. We will face situations where our need for his help is obvious—such as those that make us afraid or leave us feeling completely out of our depth. Although this should bring us to God, our perversity is such that even then we may fail to pray! Reminders of our need to turn to him will come in other ways as well. One is the possibility of tension or conflict with our partners in ministry or within our churches, for this will not be resolved properly unless God does what only he can do. Another is when people stray from the gospel or set themselves against it. Here it is obvious that we must ask God to bring them to repentance, and to fill us with his grace and truth as we relate to them. There are many other challenges or struggles in ministry that will make us aware of our need to pray.

Sadly, it is easy to miss the fact that we need God just as much when we don't feel under pressure. Whenever we read and study the Bible, we should be asking him to feed us, grow us, and change us. Whenever we teach it to others—no matter how many times we have done it before—we must ask him to help us and use us, so that his word takes root in them and bears fruit in their lives. If we are to have a real love for those we serve, we will need to ask God to grow this love in us. And one of the most important expressions of our love is to pray for each other. Our commitment to living and working for God's glory should also keep us praying, for it is only if he works with us that he will be glorified as he should be. And every day we should be thanking him for all the ways in which he is showing his goodness in our lives and ministries. So there is no excuse for praying only when I am feeling hard-pressed or overwhelmed!

The Bible makes it very clear that prayer is an essential mark of authentic Christian ministry. That is because we cannot rightly work for God unless we wait on God. Only by a steadfast reliance on him will we do his work in his way. The big question is this: are we as prayerful as we know we should be? And since the answer is bound to be "No", the next question should be: what realistic first step will I take today – looking to God for his help – to begin the process of becoming more prayerful?

Worth pondering ...

Neglect of time alone with God is the single greatest spiritual pitfall you and I face.[45]

It is certain that God's grace can bring people to heaven without our preaching: but our preaching can never bring people to heaven without God's grace; and, therefore, we should be as much in care, as much in earnest, to pray for the operations of grace, as to propose the offers of grace ...[46]

Lord God, you have placed me in your church as overseer and pastor. You see how unfit I am to administer this great and difficult office. Had I previously been without help from you, I would have ruined everything long ago. Therefore I call upon you. I gladly offer my mouth and heart to your service. I would teach the people and I myself would continue to learn. To this end I shall meditate diligently on your Word. Use me, dear Lord, as your instrument. Only do not forsake me; for if I were to continue alone, I would quickly ruin everything. Amen.[47]

The minister who does not earnestly pray over his work must surely be a vain and conceited man. He acts as if he thought himself sufficient of himself, and therefore needed not to appeal to God... The preacher who neglects to pray much must be very careless about his ministry. He cannot have comprehended his calling. He cannot have computed the value of a soul, or estimated the meaning of eternity. He must be a mere official ...[48]

The basic reason a minister must pray is not because he is a minister ... but because he is a poor, needy creature dependent on God's grace.[49]

---

[45] Reid Ferguson, The Little Book of Things You Should Know About Ministry (Christian Focus, 2002), 52.
[46] Matthew Henry, The Complete Works, 2 volumes (Baker, 1979 [1710]), 1.477.
[47] Martin Luther, Works (Concordia, 1968 [1542]), 5.123.
[48] C.H. Spurgeon, Lectures to My Students (Hendrickson, 2010 [1875]), 49.
[49] James Stewart, Heralds of God (Hodder & Stoughton, 1946), 201.

4. Christian ministry is focused ...

4.3. on some essential commitments.

One of the most crucial is the "ministry of the word".[50]

The word of God is at the heart of all authentic Christian service. That is because God does his saving, kingdom-building work with his word. So his word must be the foundation and focus of our ministries: we must always be bringing God's word to people and bringing people to God's word. Although we have already explored this theme several times, it is so important that we need to take another look at what the Bible teaches us here.

This priority is something we learn from the Lord Jesus, who gave himself above all to "the ministry of the word". This is very clear in John's Gospel, with much of chapters 5–12 taken up with Jesus' public teaching, and then chapters 13–16 devoted to his teaching of the disciples. But it is easy to miss this in Mark's Gospel, which at first glance appears to concentrate on what Jesus does. Yet even though Mark does not often record what Jesus said, a careful reading of his narrative shows that Jesus was constantly engaged in teaching all who came to him.[51] In fact, his ongoing ministry of the word was the context in which he performed the mighty works Mark often describes. Of particular importance here are the passages in which Jesus makes it clear that this is what lies at the heart of his mission: he had come to be an evangelist, a herald, a teacher, a witness.[52]

We see the same priority and focus in the ministry of the apostles.[53] In early days they made it clear that they were committed above all to prayer and the ministry of the word (Acts 6:2, 4). The result of their

---

[50] Mark 1:14, 38; 2:2, 13; 3:14; 4:14-20; 6:34; 10:1; Acts 5:42; 6:4; 18:11; 19:8-10; 2 Cor 4:1-8; 1 Tim 4:13; 5:17; 6:20-21; 2 Tim 1:13-14; 2:2, 15, 24-26; 4:2; Tit 1:9; Heb 13:7.

[51] Mark 1:14-15, 21-22, 38-39; 2:2, 13; 4:1, 33-34; 6:2, 6, 34; 8:31; 9:30-31; 10:1, 32-34; 11:17; 12:35, 38; 13:5-37; 14:49.

[52] Mark 1:38-39; Luke 4:18-19, 42-44; John 8:31, 38-40, 42, 45-47, 51; 12:46-50; 18:20, 37.

[53] Acts 2:41-42, 47; 4:1-4, 18-20, 31, 33; 5:21, 25; 5:42; 6:2, 4, 7; 8:25; 9:20-22, 28-29; 10:33–11:1.

determination not to be distracted by other important tasks was that the word of God spread and the Jerusalem church grew rapidly (Acts 6:7). When the Lord Jesus turned Paul from a persecutor into an apostle, we learn that his ministry too was to centre on the word of God.[54] This is what he gave himself to from the very beginning, and it continued to be his focus and principal activity in everything that happened from then onwards.[55] This high priority given to the ministry of God's word was undoubtedly a major factor in the remarkable growth of the early church.

The examples of Jesus and the apostles clearly demonstrate the vital importance of the word of God and the need to keep proclaiming and teaching it. One of the important things we learn from the book of Acts is that this did not apply only to the apostles, because many other believers were active in spreading the gospel and teaching churches.[56] We also see this in Paul's letters, which make it clear that the ministries of his associates centred on the word of God.[57] The New Testament shows that this was true also of those who exercised leadership in local churches.[58]

The various ministries of the word we see in the New Testament took place at a number of different levels. Like theirs, our ministries could be with individuals, with small groups, with whole congregations—and perhaps even with large assemblies or crowds. While different styles of presentation are needed in these different settings, we should have the same aim in each of them: to have God's word address people in such a way that his saving purpose is worked out in their lives as they come to Christ and grow in Christ. That is because the word of God plays a vital and indispensable role in the work of God.

---

[54] Acts 9:15; 22:15; 26:16, 20.

[55] Acts 9:20, 22, 28-29; 11:25-26; 13:1-5, 42-49; 14:1-3, 6-7, 21-27; 15:35-36; 16:10; 17:1-4, 6-7, 10-12, 17-18; 18:4-11, 27-28; 19:8-10, 20; 20:17-31; 21:17-20; 28:23-31.

[56] Acts 6:8–7:53; 8:4-5, 12, 26-40; 11:19-21; 15:32, 35, 40-41; 16:6, 10; 18:24-28.

[57] 1 Cor 4:17; 16:10; Phil 2:22; 4:2-3; Col 1:6-7; 1 Thess 3:1-3; 1 Tim 4:6, 11-16; 6:2; 2 Tim 1:13-14; 2:14-15, 24-26; 4:1-5; Tit 2:1-3, 9, 15; 3:1, 8.

[58] Acts 20:28, 30, 32; Eph 4:11; 1 Thess 5:12; 1 Tim 3:2; 5:17; 2 Tim 2:2; Tit 1:9; Heb 13:7.

It is only through the word of God that we can meet and know him.[59] It is only through the word of God that we can "grow in the grace and knowledge of our Lord and Saviour Jesus Christ" (2 Pet 3:18). It is only through the word of God that we can be "thoroughly equipped for every good work" (2 Tim 3:17; Tit 3:8). It is only from the word of God that we can learn his will and gain the wisdom we need for doing his will in daily life.[60] It is only the word of God that can make us firm and strong so that we reach our glorious inheritance as God's holy people.[61] And the word of God is the weapon which arms us against the attacks of the evil one.[62] Whenever we meet together as God's people, his word should be at the centre of what we do.[63] If we are to care for any of God's flock, the only food we have to give them is the word of God—and this is also the weapon by which we drive away any wolves that threaten them. There is much more we could say here, for it is difficult to think of any aspect of living and serving as a Christian where the Bible does not have a vital role to play.

As the word of God should be foundational in Christian life, so it must be the foundation and focus of Christian ministry. Whatever form it takes, our ministry should use the Bible as much as possible—which leaves us with an obvious but crucial question: what changes do I need to make without delay so that God's word is more central in all that I seek to do for him?

---

[59] John 17:20; Rom 15:20; 2 Cor 2:12, 14, 17; 4:3-6; Gal 3:1-3, 26-29; 4:8-9; 2 Thess 1:8; 1 John 1:1-3; 2:12-14; 4:6-16.

[60] Deut 4:5-6; 26:16-17; Psa 25:4-5, 8-10, 12, 14; 119:1-11; Isa 2:3; Jer 7:22-23; 11:1-4; John 15:10-17; Acts 20:27; Rom 6:17; Eph 4:20-24; 1 Thess 4:1-3, 8; 1 John 2:3-5; 2 John 4-6.

[61] Acts 20:32; 2 Thess 2:13-15; 1 John 2:14.

[62] Matt 4:4, 7, 10; Eph 6:17.

[63] Col 3:16; Heb 10:23-25.

Worth pondering ...

While preaching...is one form of the ministry of the Word, many other forms are reflected in the Bible and in contemporary Christian church life. It is important to grasp this point clearly, or we shall try to make preaching carry a load which it cannot bear; that is, the burden of doing all that the Bible expects of every form of ministry of the Word.[64]

[Let] pastors boldly dare all things by the word of God...let them edify the house of Christ; let them demolish the reign of Satan; let them feed the sheep, kill the wolves, instruct and exhort the docile; let them rebuke, reprove, reproach, and convince the rebel—but all through and with the word of God. But if pastors turn away from the word...they are no longer to be received as pastors, but being seen to be rather pernicious wolves, they are to be chased away. For Christ has commanded us to listen only to those who teach us that which they have taken from his word.[65]

How] can God be loved, feared or dreaded where he is not known? Or how can there be any health or eternal salvation where there is not love, fear or dread of God? And if it is life eternal ... to know God the Father and his Son Jesus Christ, then it must follow that it is death not to know God the Father and his Son Jesus Christ, and God's benefits to us for Christ's sake. These benefits are unknown where the Word of God is not taught; therefore how necessary it is ... to have the Word of God plenteously preached and truly taught, that God might be known, loved, feared and dreaded...[66]

You can't be a pastor without the Bible. You can be a life coach, a therapist, a counselor, and a negotiator without the Bible, but you cannot be a pastor.[67]

We recognize no other pastors in the church than faithful pastors of the Word of God, feeding the sheep of Jesus Christ on the one hand with instruction, admonition, consolation, exhortation, deprecation; and on the other resisting all false doctrines and deceptions of the devil, without mixing with the pure doctrine of the Scriptures their dreams or their foolish imaginings.[68]

---

[64] Peter Adam, Speaking God's Words: A Practical Theology of Preaching (IVP, 1996), 59.

[65] John Calvin, Instruction in Faith [1537] in James T. Dennison, Jr (ed), Reformed Confessions of the 16th and 17th Centuries in English Translation, Volume I, 1523-1552 (Reformation Heritage, 2008), 389.

[66] Lancelot Ridley in Graham Tomlin (ed), Philippians, Colossians, RCS: NT XI (IVP Academic, 2013), 136.

[67] Jared C. Wilson, The Pastor's Justification: Applying the Work of Christ in Your Life and Ministry (Crossway, 2013), 70.

[68] The Genevan Confession [1536] in Mark A. Noll (ed), Confessions and Catechisms of the Reformation (Baker, 1991), 131.

4. Christian ministry is focused ...

4.3. on some essential commitments.

High on the list must be loving God's people.[69]

Christian ministry is not primarily about tasks but about people. So the chief mark of faithful service is not efficiency but love! Ministry is not just a matter of getting jobs done or working out good routines and keeping to them. Yes, there are tasks to be completed, but our responsibility does not end there. We must do the right things—but we must also do them in the right way. We do not make God's word known as we should just by making public announcements to anonymous crowds. The biblical pattern goes beyond declaring the gospel: it also means engaging with people, because it is to be done in love (1 Thess 2:8). And it is not enough to love my ministry—for that might just mean that I love being in the spotlight! Ministry means serving people—and serving people means getting involved with them and giving myself to them. One of the most crucial things we learn from Jesus as the pioneer and pattern of ministry is that "serve" always goes with "give" (Mark 10:45)—and that is because "love" and "give" are partners that can't be separated.[70]

If our ministries are to be authentic, we must love those we serve. There are no exceptions here, no one we can close our hearts to. If we are to be like God our Father, we must even love our enemies, those who hate us and mistreat us.[71] But we have a particular obligation to those who are our "brothers and sisters": we are to "serve one another humbly in love" (Gal 5:13). Paul helps us to see what this means in practice in his "one another" statements, where he specifies how we should treat each other.[72] In addition to loving those we serve, we must also love those who serve

---

[69] Mark 1:14, 38; 2:2, 13; 3:14; 4:14-20; 6:34; 10:1; Acts 5:42; 6:4; 18:11; 19:8-10; 2 Cor 4:1-8; 1 Tim 4:13; 5:17; 6:20-21; 2 Tim 1:13-14; 2:2, 15, 24-26; 4:2; Tit 1:9; Heb 13:7.

[70] John 3:16; Gal 2:20; Eph 5:2.

[71] Matt 5:43-48; Luke 6:27-36; Eph 5:1.

[72] Rom 12:10, 16; 13:8; 14:13; 15:7, 14; 16:16; 1 Cor 1:10; 11:33; 12:25; Gal 5:13, 15, 26; 6:2; Eph 4:2, 25, 32; 5:19, 21; Phil 2:3-4; Col 3:9, 13, 16; 1 Thess 3:12; 4:9, 18; 5:11, 13, 15; 2 Thess 1:3; see also Heb 3:13; 10:24-25; 13:1; Jas 4:11; 5:9, 16; 1 Pet 1:22; 3:8; 4:8-9; 5:5; 1 John 1:7; 3:11.

with us. We are not just colleagues who happen to work in the same office or on the same project; we are family—and the longer we serve together, the more we should grow in our love for each other.

At one level, this is simply a matter of being Christian. Although we are called to love all of our neighbours,[73] we have a special responsibility to love our brothers and sisters.[74] When we belong to the Lord we also belong to each other, bound together as members of God's family.[75] So for us, normality is much deeper than polite arm's-length relationships. We are meant to be committed to each other, and so we should expect to develop real affection for each other. This is one of the most obvious characteristics of Paul's ministry. In his letters he frequently addresses the members of his churches as "beloved".[76] He also refers to his co-workers this way.[77] The great warmth and strong bonds involved are obvious—which is why he experiences great anguish when the relationship runs into any kind of trouble,[78] and real joy when it is working well.[79] This is pointing us to something much deeper than the rather cool and rational view of Christian love that is sometimes advocated in the western world. It is true that the real measure of our love is what we do (1 John 3:16-18)—but what we learn from Paul's ministry is that our love for each other is meant to involve not only our heads and our hands but also our hearts.[80]

At another level, serving in love means following the example set by the Lord Jesus. Like him, we should be compassionate and merciful, doing good to all.[81] But this should be true in a special way among those

---

73 Mark 12:28-34; Luke 10:25-37; Rom 13:8-10.
74 John 13:34-35; 15:12; Rom 12:9-10; Gal 5:13-15; 6:10; Eph 1:15; 4:2, 32; Phil 2:1-4; Col 1:3-4; 1 Thess 4:9-10; 2 Thess 1:3; Phm 4-7; Heb 13:1; 1 Pet 1:22; 3:8; 4:8-9; 1 John 3:11-18, 23; 4:7, 11-12, 20-21; 2 John 1-2, 5.
75 Rom 12:5; 1 Cor 12:24-26; Eph 2:19-22; 4:3-6, 25; Col 3:15; 1 Thess 4:9-10; 1 Tim 5:1-2; 1 Pet 2:17; 1 John 2:9-10; 4:20-21.
76 Rom 12:19; 1 Cor 4:14; 10:14; 15:58; 2 Cor 7:1; 12:19; Phil 2:12; 4:1; 1 Thess 2:8.
77 Rom 16:5, 8, 9, 12; 1 Cor 4:17; Eph 6:21; Col 1:7; 4:7, 9, 14; 2 Tim 1:2; Phm 1.
78 2 Cor 2:2-4; 6:11-13; 10:1–13:10; Gal 1:6-10; 4:11-20; 1 Thess 2:17–3:9; 2 Tim 1:15; 4:9-10, 16.
79 1 Cor 16:17; 2 Cor 2:3; 7:4, 7, 9, 13, 16; Phil 1:4; 2:17; 4:1, 10; Col 2:5; 1 Thess 2:19-20; 3:9; 2 Tim 1:4; Phm 7.
80 2 Cor 2:2-4; 6:11-12; 7:3; Phil 1:7-8; 1 Thess 2:17; Phm 12, 20.
81 Matt 9:36; 14:14; 15:32; 20:34; Mark 1:40-41; 10:21; Acts 10:38.

who are his followers: we are to love each other as he has loved us.[82] There is also a third angle from which we should look at this matter. This way of life means living out the gospel we proclaim: a loveless ministry would be a denial of the gospel of grace. We cannot expect people to grasp the wonder of God's costly love if we are not being transformed by it, moving steadily away from uncaring self-absorption to self-giving service.

So the Bible makes it clear that belonging to the people of God involves the obligation to love and serve each other. The New Testament has a great deal to say about what this means. We are to bear with the failings of the weak (Rom 15:1), and to please our neighbours for their good, so as to build them up (Rom 15:2). We are to restore gently any who have fallen into sin (Gal 6:1), and to carry each other's burdens (Gal 6:2). We are to consider others more important than ourselves and to reject self-seeking conduct (Phil 2:3-4). Our love is to be patient and kind, compassionate and forgiving, generous and hospitable ... and so on.[83]

It is important to see that love must be the hallmark of our ministry rather than just one of its ingredients. This follows from the fact that love is to be supreme in our lives. It is our highest responsibility (Mark 12:28-31). It is also the crowning virtue, that which unites all the others (Col 3:14; 2 Pet 1:5-7). So it is more necessary than even the most spectacular ministry-gifts (1 Cor 12:31–13:4)—and without it, all of our service would be worthless, no matter how impressive it may seem. The fruit of the Spirit—of which love is the greatest—is more important than the gifts of the Spirit.[84]

To love our fellow-believers is to imitate God-in-Christ (Eph 4:32–5:2), to live as Jesus did (1 John 2:6; 3:16). This is an essential commitment for everyone engaged in Christian ministry—and so we need to ask, am I praying and working to love my brothers and sisters in the way that God has loved me?

---

[82]   John 11:3, 5, 36; 13:1, 34-35; 15:12, 17; Eph 4:32–5:2; 1 John 3:16-18.
[83]   Rom 12:12-13; 1 Cor 13:4; 2 Cor 2:7-8; 8:1-4; Gal 5:22; Eph 4:2, 32; Phil 2:1; Col 3:12-13; 1 Thess 5:14-15; 1 Tim 5:10; 2 Tim 2:24; 1 Pet 3:8; 4:9; 2 Pet 1:7; 1 John 3:17-18; 3 John 8.
[84]   1 Cor 12:31; 13:13; 14:1, 12; Gal 5:22-23.

Worth pondering ...

To be servants of the Word it is not enough to love preaching; we have to love people. To love preaching means that we are loving our own actions... Our ministry is a means to an end, and its only value lies in the extent to which it serves the people who hear us.[85]

[If] there still are such among us as are weak, imperfect, and wayward in their faith and manners, we should deal with them in a gentle and friendly way, comforting, strengthening, admonishing, and bearing with them precisely as brothers and sisters do in a family, where one or more may be weak, imperfect, and needy. It cannot be otherwise. If we are to live together, we must put up with sundry weaknesses, grievances, and aversions. All of us cannot be equally strong in faith, disposition, talents, and blessings. There is no one who does not have many weaknesses and imperfections which he naturally expects others to bear.[86]

[The] lambs of the flock live in the love of Christ: shall they not live in ours? ...They were chosen in love; they were redeemed in love; they have been called in love; they have been washed in love; they have been fed by love, and they will be kept by love till they come to ... heaven. You and I will be out of gear with the vast machinery of divine love unless our souls are full of affectionate zeal for the good of the beloved ones...Love, and then feed.[87]

If we love the Good Shepherd, we will love his sheep and minister to them in love. If we don't truly love Jesus Christ, then we'll love ourselves and become selfish shepherds who think only of what others can do for us, not what we can do for others.[88]

---

[85] Peter Adam, Speaking God's Words: A Practical Theology of Preaching (IVP, 1996), 163.

[86] Martin Luther in Ewald Plass (ed), What Luther Says: An Anthology (Concordia, 1959), 2.826.

[87] C.H. Spurgeon, The Metropolitan Tabernacle Pulpit (Pilgrim, 1973 [1882]), 28.572.

[88] Warren W. Wiersbe & David W. Wiersbe, Ten Power Principles for Christian Service: Ministry Dynamics for a New Century (Baker, 1997), 35.

4. Christian ministry is focused ...

4.3. on some essential commitments.

Also important is setting a godly example.[89]

Christian ministry is about what we are as well as what we do. It is not only about our competence; it is also about our character. So when Paul speaks about assessing someone's suitability to hold a ministry position, it is striking that he focuses primarily on how that person lives.[90] It is not that the work to be done is unimportant, for Paul gives it great emphasis.[91] But it is vitally important that those who do this work are fit to do so—and what gets them fit is their training regime: they are to be training themselves in godliness (1 Tim 4:7-8). So our role or position—pastor, youth worker, or whatever it might be—cannot be defined only in terms of our tasks or activities. Yes, we must seek to impart the word of God to all those we serve, but we cannot stop there. We are also to set them an example of growing godliness.

This was an important part of Paul's ministry as a pioneer missionary and church-planter. He was well aware that he not only needed to teach converts about new life in Christ but also needed to model it for them (1 Cor 4:17). So what they saw as he worked amongst them was not haphazard but deliberate, a pattern of life and ministry he wanted them to see and follow. It is because he intended to set an example for them that his letters call on them to imitate him.[92] This was also an important aspect of the training he gave his co-workers: as they saw his life and ministry at close quarters, their own lives were given shape and direction (Phil 3:17; 2 Tim 3:10-11). And he expected these co-workers in their turn to set an example for their churches (1 Tim 4:12; Tit 2:7-8). They had to practice what they preached, so that their hearers could practice what they

---

[89] 1 Cor 4:16-17; 10:32–11:1; Phil 3:17; 4:9; 1 Thess 1:5-6; 2:10-12; 2 Thess 3:6-9; 1 Tim 4:12; Tit 2:7; 1 Pet 5:3.

[90] 1 Tim 3:1-13; Tit 1:6-9. Also relevant are 1 Tim 4:6-8, 11-16; 6:11-15; 2 Tim 2:15-16, 22-26; 2:7-8.

[91] 1 Tim 3:9; 4:6, 11, 13-16; 5:17; 6:11-13, 20-21; 2 Tim 1:13-14; 2:2, 14-16, 24-26; 3:14–4:5; Tit 1:9-11; 2:1, 7-8, 13; 3:8-9.

[92] 1 Cor 4:16, 11:1; Phil 3:17; 4:9; 2 Thess 3:7, 9.

were taught. Some of these would be leaders in the particular church involved, and they too were to live exemplary lives. Anyone who shepherds God's sheep must be an example for them (1 Pet 5:3).

Our responsibility to set an example for those we serve means that our lives and ministries must display integrity. The first and most important reason for this is that we are accountable to the Lord: we live and serve before him, in his presence and under his scrutiny.[93] But there is another reason for taking this seriously: there is a direct and obvious link between the integrity of our lives and the cogency of our teaching. If our conduct is clearly at odds with what the Bible teaches, why should our hearers take our message seriously? It will be hard to convince them that there is new life in Christ if we are not living that new life. Why would they embrace "the gospel of grace", "the word of truth", if they see no grace and truth in us?[94] There must be consistency between what we teach and how we live and serve, so that the gospel is not hindered or discredited.

While we must take this responsibility seriously, we must not take it further than the Bible does. What we are to model is not something superior or out of the ordinary but the conduct that should characterise all believers.[95] There is no suggestion in the Bible that what puts leaders in a position to set an example is that they have arrived at an advanced level of godliness. What others are meant to see in us is a work in progress rather than a finished product (1 Tim 4:15). We are to model growth—a growing devotion to Christ and a growing likeness to Christ (Phil 3:8-17). This is what we should be doing anyway, for this is an essential part of Christian discipleship: along with every other believer, we must continue to "grow in the grace and knowledge of our Lord and Saviour Jesus Christ" (2 Pet 3:18). But this is also what we owe to those we serve and lead: by our steadily growing faithfulness and maturity, we must point the way forward and encourage them to follow it.[96]

---

93 Rom 1:9; 2 Cor 2:17; 4:2; 8:21; 12:19; Gal 1:20; Phil 1:8; 1 Thess 2:3-5, 10; 1 Tim 5:21; 6:13; 2 Tim 2:14; 4:1.
94 Acts 14:3; 20:24, 32; Eph 1:13; Col 1:5, NASB; 2 Tim 2:15; Jas 1:18.
95 1 Tim 4:12; 6:11-14; 2 Tim 2:20-24; 3:10-14; Tit 2:2-8; 3:1-2, 8.
96 1 Tim 4:12; 2 Tim 2:19-22; Tit 2:7-8; 1 Pet 5:3.

What will it be like for everyone to see our progress (1 Tim 4:15)? When we are pressing on as we should (Phil 3:12-14), two things will be evident to those we serve. The first is our determination not to stagnate but to keep growing as a Christian. This will show itself in two ways that belong together. We will rely on God to do what only he can do—and we will also give ourselves to doing what we must do. The Bible makes it clear that Christian growth must involve both. For example, if I am to be pure in heart (Psa 24:3-4; Matt 5:8) I will have to ask God to create this heart in me (Psa 51:10) and I will also have to cleanse my heart (Jas 4:8). If people are to see our progress, we will need to keep asking God to do his transforming work in our lives, making us new by producing in us the fruit of the Spirit.[97] At the same time, we will need to keep obeying the Bible's call to "make every effort" to develop a more godly character.[98] The likeness to Jesus that is God's purpose for us (Rom 8:29) will require God to change us to be like him (2 Cor 3:18) and will also require us to set ourselves to be like him (1 John 2:6).

That is only one side of the story, however. It is also true that "we all stumble in many ways" (Jas 3:2). So another essential part of setting a godly example is the way we deal with faults and failures, in others and in ourselves. Do we magnify the grace of God and the cross of Christ, not only in our teaching but also in the way that we deal with such wrongs, both theirs and ours? Is it obvious that we are relying not on a God who relates only to the virtuous, but on the God of the gospel, who pardons and sets his love on deeply-flawed rebels? Do we make this obvious by admitting our wrongdoings, and doing what we can to put things right when we have failed? Do we make it clear that our confidence before God does not lie in any good that we might do but only in the perfect work that the Lord Jesus has done for us? And do we respond to the flaws and wrongs of others with the same forbearance and readiness to forgive that God shows to us? In other words, is it plain to see, in this respect as in every other, that our lives and ministries are firmly grounded in the gospel?

If we have been entrusted with a ministry, we must watch both our life and our doctrine closely (1 Tim 4:16). We must take as much care to get our

---

[97] 2 Cor 4:16; Gal 5:22-23; Col 3:10.
[98] Rom 14:19; Eph 4:2; Heb 12:14; 2 Pet 1:5, 10; 3:14.

life and ministry right as we take to get our teaching right. We should be praying and working for a steadily growing godliness of character that will serve as an example to the flock. So I need to ask myself quite often whether my life points people in the same direction as my teaching – and what disparities need serious attention straight away.

Worth pondering ...

Take heed to yourselves, lest your example contradict your doctrine...lest you unsay with your lives, what you say with your tongues...It is a palpable error of some ministers, who make such a disproportion between their preaching and their living; who study hard to preach exactly, and study little or not at all to live exactly...if we will be the servants of Christ indeed, we must not be tongue servants only, but must serve him with our deeds... Take heed to yourselves, lest you are weak though your own negligence, and lest you mar the work of God by your weakness.[99]

When we set about teaching others we must first allow ourselves to be taught. For if we are reluctant to learn and thus to grow in understanding so that others may grow with us, we cannot fulfil our task. Therefore the person whom God has established as teacher and instructor in his house must himself be the first pupil, and must be all the more ready to receive teaching and admonition.[100]

Sincerity, consistency and reliability: failure to demonstrate integrity in these ways is quite possibly the most serious obstacle in any form of Christian ministry and, indeed, in the growth of God's work.[101]

You cannot read too much in Scripture; and what you read you cannot read too carefully, and what you read carefully you cannot understand too well, and what you understand well you cannot teach too well, and what you teach well you cannot live too well.[102]

A pastor's life should be vocal; sermons must be practiced as well as preached...If a man teach uprightly and walk crookedly, more will fall down in the night of his life than he built in the day of his doctrine.[103]

---

99 Richard Baxter, The Reformed Pastor (Banner of Truth, 1974 [1656]), 63, 64, 71.
100 John Calvin, Sermons on Titus (Banner of Truth, 2015 [1561]), 75 [on 1:7-9].
101 Jonathan Lamb, Integrity: Leading with God Watching (IVP, 2006), 34.
102 Martin Luther, quoted in Thomas C. Oden, Becoming a Minister (Crossroad, 1987), 165.
103 John Owen, Works (Banner of Truth, 1967 [1647]), 13.57.

4. Christian ministry is focused ...

4.3. on some essential commitments.

These must include persevering through hardships.[104]

Christian ministry will often be tough going. It can involve many hurts and hardships, many tears and trials. Some of these will be the result of our own sins and failures, while some will be due to the faults and errors of those we work with. Then there are those that are likely to come from opposition to our message or ministry, either from an unfaithful church or from a hostile world. So ministry is not for the faint-hearted. We will need to be tenacious and persevering, determined not to lose heart or give up.

Such a prospect is bound to make us wonder how we will cope—or even whether we will survive. And sooner or later, it will face us with the question, is ministry worth it? Why persist with something that involves so much trouble and hardship? If we are going to handle these questions well, our ministry must be built on strong foundations. We will need to have a clear grasp of the fundamentals. So what have we learned so far that we will need to keep front and centre?

If we are going to respond well to tough times in ministry, we will need above all to be centred steadfastly on the Lord Jesus himself. This will mean reminding myself often that ministry starts with him, the pioneer of ministry. I am serving him only because he has first served me—and in serving and saving me, he held nothing back and went all the way down. If he was prepared to pay such a terrible price for me, could I not take a few knocks and bear a few wounds for him?

I also need to remember that he is the pattern for ministry—and so it is my calling to follow him along the path of humble, sacrificial service. But if I am to follow in his steps, I must keep recalling the example he set in his sufferings (1 Pet 2:21-23). If I am not to grow weary or lose heart, I must consider how he endured great shame and strong opposition from

---

[104] Mark 13:12-13; 1 Cor 4:12; 2 Cor 6:4-10; 1 Thess 1:6; 2:2, 9; 2 Tim 1:8; 2:3, 10; 3:10-11; 4:5; Heb 10:32-36; 12:1-3; Jas 1:12.

sinners (Heb 12:2-3). To develop perseverance in my ministry I will need to reflect often on the perseverance he showed in his (2 Thess 3:5).

I can train myself to be steadfast in the face of trouble by continuing to recognize that it is a great privilege to serve the Lord. I should make it my practice to thank him regularly for giving me a place in the work he is doing—which will also remind me frequently that I have a ministry only because of his grace. It is obvious that the right response to a generous giver is not grumbling but gratitude—so it is vital that I keep looking at my ministry as God's gift to me. The more clearly I see this, the more likely I am to cope with the rough patches. It takes real tenacity to persevere through the hardships that ministry might bring me—and the best generator of the grit I need is the grace of God!

This brings us to another of the fundamental principles we have considered: because God includes me in what he is doing, I must do his work in his way. That means learning to rely on the Holy Spirit in every part of my ministry. If I have been doing this every day, asking him to supply all that I lack and to work with me and through me, I have been facing the fact that I am not meant to manage on my own. This will mean that I am more likely to turn to him quickly when things go wrong, to ask for the help that only he can give. I should be thoroughly convinced that the Spirit excels at empowering the weak, at encouraging the downhearted, at emboldening the fearful—and thus at enabling us to endure through tough times.

What we are talking about here is not limited to those in ministry positions, for every Christian has to learn how to persevere through hardships. One of the keys here is holding fast to the promises of God—or better still, holding fast to the God of the promises. He has given us many rock-solid guarantees that are meant to make our trust in him more steadfast and enduring. We can be certain that he will never abandon us (Heb 13:5) or test us beyond our ability to endure (1 Cor 10:13); that he will do good in and with everything that happens to us, especially by making us more like Jesus (Rom 8:28-29); that nothing will separate us from his love (Rom 8:37-39) or pluck us from his grasp (John 10:28-29).

In addition to such promises as these—and the Bible has many more like them—he has also given us wonderful assurances about our ministries. We know that he can and will use us, despite all of the ways in which we are weak and flawed.[105] He has given his word that what we do for him will never be forgotten or turn out to be fruitless.[106] And at the End, he will wipe away every tear that our ministries have caused and overwhelm all of their griefs and pains with a tsunami of everlasting joy.[107] Because God is utterly faithful to his promises,[108] those promises, treasured and trusted, are likely to make us faithful too.

As well as God's promises, we also have godly examples to encourage us to persevere under trial. The Bible contains many accounts of people who served the Lord without giving up, despite facing ordeals that were often extreme.[109] They are the large cloud of witnesses who now surround us as we take our turn in the great race that requires us to be persevering and firmly focused on Jesus (Heb 12:1-2).

Church history too is full of examples of faithful service under duress of many kinds. This is not confined to the past, of course: it would be surprising if we did not know believers who display the kind of steadfast endurance we should imitate. It is also quite likely that at least some of the ministries from which we have benefited have involved hardships that had to be endured—which means that they have modelled how we are meant to serve.

It is important not to get things out of balance here, as can easily happen when we are having a really hard time. The trials that come our way are never the whole story. There is no escaping the fact that dark canyons will be part of the journey—but so will the oases (Psa 23:2, 4). And not only will the good Shepherd stay with us in the canyons, but his goodness and love will be hot on our heels every day (Psa 23:6).

Christian ministry means following our Servant-Lord, who for our sake endured constant temptation and trials, opposition and rejection,

---

[105] 1 Cor 1:27-29; 2:3-5; 2 Cor 4:7-11, 16; 11:30; 12:7b-10; Gal 4:13-14; Eph 3:13; 6:19-20; 2 Tim 4:16-17; Jas 3:1-2.

[106] 2 Chron 15:7; Prov 19:17; Jer 31:16; Mark 9:41; John 15:16; Acts 10:31; 1 Cor 3:8; 15:58; Eph 6:7-8; Col 3:23-24; Heb 6:10.

[107] Pss 16:11; Isa 51:11; Matt 5:11-12; 1 Thess 2:19-20; Rev 7:17; 21:4.

[108] Num 23:19; Josh 21:45; 23:14; 1 Kgs 8:56; Psa 145:13; Heb 10:23; 11:11.

[109] Acts 5:40-41; 7:54–8:3; 20:18-19, 22-24; Eph 3:13; Phil 1:29-30; Col 1:24; 1 Thess 1:6; 2:2, 14-16; 2 Thess 1:3-7, 11-12; 2 Tim 1:8; 2:8-10; 3:10-12; 4:14-17; Heb 6:11-12; 11:32–12:1; Jas 5:10-11.

then betrayal and brutality, and finally all of the terrible agonies of the cross. While these sufferings went far, far beyond anything we might face, serving him in this sinful world is bound to involve hardships, and we must learn to bear them for his sake. Since he persevered through all of this in order to serve and save us, we should be committed to persevering through any and every hardship as we serve him, confident that he will hold us fast and bring us through.

Worth pondering ...

Like the gospel, ministry gifts are freely given, but are costly to receive.[110]

[That] one so exalted as Christ himself, the only and eternal Son of God, has trod the path of suffering before us, enduring unlimited distress, agony transcending the power of humanity to experience—this alone should be enough to admonish and urge anyone to patiently endure affliction. Why, then, should we disciples, we who are so insignificant and inexperienced in comparison with our Master—why should we be at all troubled at any suffering for his sake? Especially when all he asks of us is to follow him, to learn of him and to remain his disciples.[111]

All pastoral afflictions are graciously designed to make us rely on God and not ourselves. And therefore our afflictions prepare us to do the one thing most needful for our people—to point them away from ourselves to the all-sufficient God.[112]

Only deep gratitude for a suffering Savior can make a man willing to suffer in ministry. It is only a heart that is satisfied in Christ that can be spiritually content in the hardships of ministry.[113]

---

[110] Peter Adam, "The Pastor as Preacher" in Melvin Tinker (ed), The Renewed Pastor: Essays on the Pastoral Ministry in Honour of Philip Hacking (Mentor, 2011), 67-82 (at 69).

[111] Martin Luther, Sermons (Baker, 1983), 7.252f.

[112] John Piper, Brothers, We Are Not Professionals: A Plea to Pastors for Radical Ministry, updated and expanded (B&H, 2013), 167.

[113] Paul David Tripp, Dangerous Calling: The Unique Challenges of Pastoral Ministry (IVP, 2012), 64.

4. Christian ministry is focused ...

4.4. on some crucial tasks.

These are evangelism: winning the lost;[114] discipling: establishing and equipping new believers;[115] caring for the flock, especially the most needy;[116] and training new workers.[117]

There are several major dimensions of Christian ministry, activities that should have a high priority in all that we are doing. In some ways the most basic is the role of the fisherman, to which Jesus called his disciples (Mark 1:17; Luke 5:8-11). If no fishing is being done, there will be no flock to pastor! Because Jesus had appointed them to fish for people, evangelism was a vital part of the ministry of the twelve apostles.[118] But the book of Acts shows that it was by no means confined to them, as many believers were active in evangelism.[119] It was also fundamental to the role of the great missionary pioneer Paul (Rom 15:20; 1 Cor 1:17)—and it was also to feature in the ministry of those who, like Timothy, served in the local church. Timothy may not have been gifted as an evangelist (Eph 4:11), but Paul expected him to "do the work of an evangelist" (2 Tim 4:5). His ministry of the word of God should not remain within the confines of the church; he should be getting the gospel into the public domain, seeking to lead people to turn to the Lord and entrust themselves to him.

This should be part of my ministry too. The most obvious reason for this is that I am a Christian! Every believer must be seeking to make the gospel known to those who are without Christ. How could we think that we have truly loved our neighbours if we have not given them the word of life, the gospel of salvation? And how could we think that we have truly loved the Lord if we have not been using (or creating!) every opportunity

---

114 1 Cor 9:22; 10:31-33; 2 Cor 5:18-20; 2 Tim 4:5.

115 Matt 28:19-20; 1 Thess 2:11-12; 3:2, 10; 4:1-2; 2 Tim 2:24-26; Tit 2:1-10; 2 Pet 1:10-12; 3:1-2, 17-18.

116 Matt 25:34-40; Acts 20:28, 34-35; 2 Cor 1:3-7; 1 Thess 2:7-12; 3:2-3; 1 Tim 5:3, 16; Jas 2:14-17; 1 Pet 5:2-3; 1 John 3:16-18; 3 John 5-8.

117 Phil 2:22; 2 Tim 1:13-14; 2:2; 3:10-14.

118 Acts 2:5-41; 3:11-26; 4:8-12, 33; 5:18-21, 42; 8:25; 10:24-48.

119 Acts 6:10-14; 8:4-5, 26-35, 40; 11:19-21; 15:36-39; 18:24-28; 21:8.

to speak the word that shows his worth: the gospel of the glory of Christ and the grace of God? There is another reason this should belong to my ministry: if I want the people I serve to be committed to evangelism, I need to set them an example. This will need to be part of what I am doing as a trainer, the fourth of the roles we are considering.

Then there is the role of the discipler, establishing new believers in the Christian life. This has much in common with the roles of the teacher (Matt 28:19-20) and the shepherd. Discipling new-born Christians means grounding them in the word of God in the way a teacher does. They will need to have a clear grasp of the gospel, so that they build their lives on the grace of God and thus keep growing in their love for him. They will also need a growing understanding of what the Bible tells us about the will of God, so that they live in glad obedience to him. Such teaching is vitally important, but it is not sufficient. Discipling new believers also involves caring for them as a shepherd, that is, a pastor. They will need to be supported and encouraged, warned against "the sin that so easily entangles" (Heb 12:1), and helped to get back on their feet when they have tripped up. I will need to show them how to pray and feed on God's word every day, how to give and receive in Christian fellowship, how to share the gospel with others, how to be wise in their stewardship of all that God has given them—and much else besides. I should also be equipping them to serve others. In most cases, they will learn best if I give them suitable opportunities to do it with me.

Some of the teaching and pastoring that discipling involves can be done in groups, but some of it is best done one-to-one. Even if I could manage to do it all, it is good to involve others in this important work. At first, many will need to do it with me so that they can learn how to do it— but my aim should be to get them to the point where they can do it without me. Here too I will be working as a trainer.

There is the role of the shepherd, feeding and caring for the flock.[120] Again, this is not only the responsibility of church-planters like Paul; it is also for those who lead the local church.[121] Yet pastors and elders do not have a monopoly here, for this is an important element of our fellowship

---

[120] John 21:15-17; Acts 20:28; Eph 4:11; 1 Pet 5:2-3.
[121] 1 Thess 5:12; 1 Tim 1:3-5; 3:14-15; 4:12-16.

as believers. So even though he refers to the ministry of their leaders (1 Thess 5:12-13), Paul expects all of the Thessalonians to be involved in what we would call pastoral care (1 Thess 4:18; 5:11, 14-15). This is a regular feature of what the New Testament says about church life.[122] Such mutual interaction happens most naturally in a house-church (what we would call a home group), whose leader would have responsibility for shepherding its members. Those who are the leaders of the whole church are its shepherds, keeping watch over all the flock (Acts 20:28). So when a church is functioning as it should, pastoring will be happening at several levels. But it is important that some—the elders or pastors, who are also called "overseers" in the New Testament—have oversight of the whole body.[123] This should ensure that no one is overlooked, and that those with special needs and heavy burdens receive the care and support they need. This is one of the most important responsibilities of the shepherd (Ezek 34:2-4).

Then there is the role of the trainer, equipping and coaching new workers. We see this in Jesus' ministry, as he devoted lots of time and effort to preparing the disciples for their future role as his apostles.[124] It was also a prominent feature of Paul's ministry. His letters name a great many people he involved in his work and who would have therefore learned about ministry from him. This applied especially to Timothy, who travelled for long periods as part of Paul's team and was also sent on various assignments, some of them quite demanding.[125] Paul tells Timothy that he is to pass the baton to suitable people, so that they will do the same (2 Tim 2:2). In this way there will be a steady stream of competent people committed to the work of the gospel. We should be doing what we can to ensure that this stream does not dry up when our ministry is over but keeps getting stronger all the time.

---

[122] Rom 12:10, 13, 15-18; Gal 5:13-15, 26; 6:1-2; Eph 4:2-3, 16; 5:18-21; Phil 2:1-4; Col 3:12-16; Heb 10:24-25; 1 Pet 1:22; 3:8; 4:8-10.

[123] This overseeing is referred to in Acts 20:28; Phil 1:1; 1 Tim 3:1-2; Tit 1:7; 1 Pet 5:2.

[124] Mark 3:13-19; 4:10-20, 34; 6:7-13, 30-31; 7:17-22; 8:27-33; 9:28-37; 10:10-12, 23-45; 14:12-31; 16:7; Luke 24:36-49; John 13:1–17:26; 20:17-29; 21:15-19.

[125] Acts 16:1-5; 17:14-15; 18:5; 19:22; 20:1-5; Rom 16:21; 1 Cor 4:17; 16:10-11; 2 Cor 1:1, 19; Phil 1:1; 2:19-23; Col 1:1; 1 Thess 1:1; 3:2-3, 6; 2 Thess 1:1; 1 Tim 1:3-4, 18-19; 2 Tim 1:6- 8, 13-14; 3:10-14; 4:9-13.

Which of these four aspects of ministry receives the greatest emphasis and attention will vary according to the situation. But authentic Christian ministry will always have a place for all of them as we engage in God's wide work of mission: reaching the world, and his deep work of maturity: growing the church.

Worth pondering ...

God did not give us his word so that it might merely beat on our ears...He intends it to be food for us and to shape our lives...Just as our bodies are kept in good condition thanks to regular nourishment, so our souls are maintained by sound doctrine, which serves not only as food but as medicine...It restores us when we are sick and keeps us healthy, so that we may have the strength to engage in God's service...God's word must be used to instruct men in such a way that they are equipped to serve him.[126]

[The] pastor is also a trainer. His job is not just to provide spiritual services, nor is it his job to do all of the ministry. His task is to teach and train his congregation, by his word and his life, to become disciple-making disciples of Jesus.[127]

Leadership in the church has a twofold function, both elements equal in importance. One element focuses on task, fulfilling purposes, getting jobs done, and accomplishing goals. The other element focuses on relationships, maintaining fellowship, harmony, and cohesiveness within the body. It is destructive to favor one at the expense of the other.[128]

The pastor is simply an under-shepherd of the great Shepherd...The pastoral function issues from and is sustained by two relationships—the pastor's love for his Master, and the Master's love for His sheep...In other words, it is on the truth that Jesus Christ is Lord that the pastoral ministry is dependent and, therefore, it is by the proclamation of this truth that the pastoral ministry is safeguarded.[129]

---

[126] John Calvin, Sermons on Titus (Banner of Truth, 2015 [1561]), 155 [on 2:1-3].
[127] Colin Marshall & Tony Payne, The Trellis and the Vine: The Ministry Mind-Shift that Changes Everything (Matthias, 2009), 99.
[128] James E. Means, Leadership in Christian Ministry (Baker, 1989), 13.
[129] Daniel T. Niles, The Preacher's Calling to be Servant (Lutterworth, 1959), 56.

4. Christian ministry is focused ...

4.5. on God's glory.

We must not be self-seeking, engaged in self-promotion.[130] Rather, we should do everything for God's glory.[131] And we must not glory in our gifts or ministries; we must glory in God himself.[132]

Why do we engage in Christian ministry? What should be our motive? This is a question with several right answers. We should give ourselves to serving the Lord out of deep gratitude that he gave himself to serve and save us. We should serve because we are not our own, but belong to him who bought us by giving himself for us.[133] Since we should share God's love for the world (John 3:16), we should serve out of love for those who are lost, who are in dire need of the word of life, the gospel of salvation. We should also share Christ's love for the church (Eph 5:25), and should therefore serve out of love for his people, who need to be guided and guarded so that we all reach maturity in Christ and enter his heavenly kingdom. All of these motives are right and necessary, and our service would not be properly Christian without them. But there is one that is even more fundamental and important than all of them.

The overriding aim in all of our service should be the glory of God. That is why God himself is at work in the world and in the church: to display his all-surpassing excellence and thus to magnify his name.[134] His great goal is to fill the earth with the knowledge of his glory (Hab 2:14). When this happens at the End, what is true on earth will at last match what is always true in heaven, as the open display of the glory of God will evoke the unending and adoring praise of us all. Because we are privileged to have a place in it, this great purpose and work of God gives

---

[130] Psa 115:1; Jer 45:5a; 1 Cor 13:4-5; 2 Cor 4:5; 5:15; 10:12-18; 11:16–12:10.
[131] Psa 115:1; Rom 15:5-7; 1 Cor 6:20; 10:31; Eph 3:20-21; Phil 1:20; 4:19-20; 2 Thess 1:11- 12; 1 Pet 4:11; 2 Pet 3:18.
[132] Psa 37:4; 43:4; 66:2; 105:3; 106:47; Isa 41:16; 61:10; Rom 5:11; 15:17; 1 Cor 1:28-31; Phil 3:3; 4:4.
[133] 1 Cor 6:19-20; 2 Cor 5:15.
[134] Ex 9:16; 1 Sam 12:22; 2 Sam 7:23; Psa 106:7-8; Isa 48:9-11; 63:11-14; Ezek 36:20-23; Matt 6:9; John 12:28; 1 John 2:12.

us the focus of our lives and the agenda for our ministries. That is why the Lord Jesus taught us to give first place in our praying to God's name and kingdom and will (Matt 6:9-10). Our greatest commitment must be to do all things for the sake of his name (Rom 1:5; 3 John 7), all for his glory.

Here is where we face one of the subtle traps in Christian ministry. The serving that is meant to put us down low can lift us up high. That is because it often puts us up front, so that we are noticed. And when people benefit from our ministry, they will express gratitude and praise. This is a very heady wine that can quickly become addictive! In no time at all, we can come to expect it and to count it as our right. If it keeps coming, we can treat our popularity—and not our faithfulness—as the measure of our ministry's worth. This is only a small step from acting in ways that make it more likely that we will be praised and popular. Our ministry thus ends up being controlled by what the "customers" want, and not by the will and word of God. In view of this danger, our motto must always be, "Not to us, but to your name be the glory" (Psa 115:1).

This motto is needed in view of another trap that ministry can involve. Where praise and popularity are common, power is not far away. That is, people's readiness to accept and value my ministry means that I am having an influence in their lives. It is not difficult for this to turn into influence over their lives—something else that can become addictive quite quickly. It is all too easy for my words and actions to become ways of wielding power rather than instruments of humble service. This should not be so among us (Mark 10:42-44), but it has been so too often—and will continue to be so unless we put in place measures that make it as difficult as possible for us to end up misusing our position like this.

Popularity and power are two of the major sources of pride—and the Bible makes it clear that pride is a most destructive force. We must therefore be active in combatting not only pride itself but also everything that can take us there. And how are we to do this? What can prevent us being trapped by these serious pitfalls? We must make it our practice to "glory in his holy name" (Psa 105:3). That is, we must keep going to the Bible to learn what God is like—and then we must keep coming to him to respond to all that he has revealed about who he is (which is what the Bible means by his "name"). This will mean staying focused on him in a way that brings us to bow before him more humbly, praise him more joyfully, rely on him more steadfastly, and obey him more wholeheartedly. But this will not happen unless the Bible is growing our understanding of his awesome majesty and unsurpassable excellency as God—and that will happen only if we keep taking in and chewing over what it tells us about him. When we do, the way we respond to him will become stronger and deeper and truer. As the Bible makes the glory of his "name" clearer to us, giving him glory in our praise and our service will increasingly be not just what we ought to do but what we long to do. At the same time, we will become steadily smaller in our own eyes as our awareness of his greatness keeps growing. This will make it harder and harder to steal for ourselves any of the glory that belongs to him.

This is one of the most important things we learn from Jesus, who was intent upon glorifying the Father in everything he said and did. He took great care to ensure that his ministry honoured the Father's primacy, making clear that all of it was rooted in what the Father gave him.[135] He also maintained an unswerving obedience to his Father's will, even in the face of terrible suffering.[136] He never went looking for a glory of his own, promoting himself in a way that siphoned off glory that should have gone to the Father. Instead, he was content with the glory his Father gave him.[137] This selfless devotion to the Father's glory provides a model for us: we are to have "the same mindset as Christ Jesus" (Phil 2:5); we "must live as Jesus did" (1 John 2:6).

Despite all of the ways in which I am tempted to put myself in the centre, authentic Christian ministry is to be relentlessly focused on God and his glory. How do I get to be like this? By soaking myself in the Bible's presentation of the glory of God so that it leads me to glory in him—and the more I glory in him, the less likely I am to deflect glory from him. Instead, I will increasingly devote what I have and am to the fame of his name, pushing harder all the time to bring honour to him in all I say and do. After all, nothing in my ministry is really about me: I serve God's

---

[135] Matt 11:27; 20:23; 21:38-43; 24:36; 26:29, 53; 28:18; John 4:23; 5:19-20, 22-23, 26-27, 36, 45; 6:37; 7:16; 8:26, 40; 10:18, 29, 32; 12:49-50; 13:16; 14:6, 10, 24, 28, 31; 15:1, 10, 15; 17:2, 5-9, 24; 20:17.

[136] Matt 4:7-10; 6:9-10; 26:39, 42; John 4:34; 5:30; 6:38; 7:18; 8:29, 49-50; 12:27-28; 17:4; 18:11.

[137] Matt 16:27; John 6:27; 8:54; 17:5, 22, 24.

people and God's world with God's word, on the basis of the gifts he has given and the strength he supplies. As in our salvation, so also in our service: "from him and through him and to him are all things. To him be the glory forever!" (Rom 11:36).

Worth pondering ...

It is so easy to seek our own glory and the increase of our own reputation, and gospel ministry is as easy a place to do that as any. Because our sinful nature is naturally proud and self-centred, we will have to battle against this and live a life of ongoing repentance in this area...The glory of God is the thing of absolute value and undiminishing worth. If we can see...that God's reputation is all-important, we will learn to spend ourselves in service of his reputation and not our own. What is our driving ambition; what do we hope to achieve in our ministry? Is it the increase of our own glory, or the increase of the Lord's?[138]

No one may seek for nor ascribe to himself power and honor because of his office and gifts. Power and glory belong only to God. He himself calls his Church, and rules, sanctifies and preserves it through his Word and Spirit. To this end he bestows upon us his gifts. And all is done purely of grace, wholly for the sake of his beloved Son, Christ the Lord. Therefore, in return for the favor and ineffable goodness bestowed upon us regardless of our merits, we ought to thank and praise God, directing all our efforts to the recognition and glory of his name.[139]

The highest of all missionary motives is neither obedience to the Great Commission (important as that is), nor love for sinners who are alienated and perishing (strong as that incentive is, especially when we contemplate the wrath of God...), but rather zeal—burning and passionate zeal—for the glory of Jesus Christ.[140]

The glories of being right, successful, in control, esteemed, and secure often become more influential in the way that ministry is done than the awesome realities of the presence, sovereignty, power, and love of God. Many pastors have lost their awe...It is the awesome glory of God's existence, character, plan, presence, promises, and grace that gives me reason to work hard and not give up [141]

---

[138] Jonathan Griffiths, The Ministry Medical: A Health-Check from 2 Timothy (Christian Focus, 2013), 135.

[139] Martin Luther, Sermons (Baker, 1983), 7.328.

[140] John Stott, The Message of Romans, BST (IVP, 1994), 53 [on 1:5].

[141] Paul David Tripp, Dangerous Calling: The Unique Challenges of Pastoral Ministry (IVP, 2012), 120f, 123f.

AND NOW?

Just as the Introduction aimed at answering important questions you might well have been asking about this book, this final section responds to two obvious questions you are likely to have now that you have finished reading it.

Have we covered everything I need to know about Christian ministry?

There are two apparently contradictory ways of answering this question. The first must be, "No." The Introduction prepared you for this answer by telling you about the ministry map which the book expounds point-by-point: "It does not try to cover everything, but seeks to identify and explain the fundamental elements of what the Bible tells us. In other words, it is meant to give you a big picture view of Christian ministry ..." So I have not tried to say everything that it would be good to say about Christian service, but have aimed at being comprehensive enough to capture all of the essentials. If a map is to help me find my way around, it cannot be so detailed that it is difficult to get a clear idea of the layout of the area it covers—but it needs to be detailed enough for me keep finding it useful. And that is what I have been aiming at: the "just right!" that lies between "too much" and "not enough".

You are likely to have noticed that there are some important aspects of Christian service that receive little or no attention in the book. One of the most obvious is the crucial matter of Christian character: the qualities that have a prominent place in the New Testament descriptions of those who are suitable to hold specific ministry roles in churches.[1] Where we tend to give priority to tasks and skills and formal qualifications, the New Testament is more concerned about real and growing godliness, which involves putting away sinful habits as well as replacing them with the Spirit's fruit and thus becoming more like Jesus. While we have considered some of these essential qualities, we have not gone deep

---

[1] 1 Tim 3:1-12; 4:6-16; 6:11-12, 20-21; 2 Tim 2:14-26; Tit 1:6-9; 2:7-8, 15; 3:9.

enough or wide enough to cover them adequately. Much the same can be said about some other significant aspects of Christian ministry.

Despite this "No", there is an important sense in which the right answer to your question is, "Yes." This becomes clear once we supply the "so that" addition needed to complete the question. The reason that you and I and all believers need to know about Christian ministry is so that we can be what we should be and do what we should do as servants of the Lord Jesus. And what we have learned by working our way through the ministry map is more than enough to enable you to make a start or to keep going in whatever field of service God has entrusted to you—and this brings us to another question you might be asking at this point.

What should I do with what I have discovered by reading this book?

It all depends on your reason for reading it. Perhaps you have done so out of general interest, without any specific need or purpose in mind. If so, I hope you have learned some helpful things about what Christian ministry is and why it matters—but it wouldn't be right to stop there. The best way I can make the next step clear is to reminisce a little.

Not long after I became a Christian, I was introduced to these words: "Only one life; it will soon be past—only what's done for Christ will last." It wasn't hard to get the message: "You only get one go at life here, so don't waste it on what doesn't matter. Make sure you use it for Jesus!" Back then I thought this meant that we should all be missionaries—and if we weren't quite brave enough for that, we should at least become full-time church workers. But I now see that this was only half-right. Where it was right was recognizing that every Christian needs to ask this one essential question: "How can I make my life count most for the sake of Jesus?" Where I went wrong was in thinking that there is only one right answer to that question.

My answer may well be quite different from yours—but this doesn't mean that only one of them can be right. The Bible does not teach, "We all have the same Lord—and so we should all serve in the same way." Instead, it tells us, "There are different kinds of service, but the same Lord" (1 Cor 12:5). So there isn't just one answer we all should give—and some of us should not give just one answer. The right answer early in my

Christian life might not be the right answer twenty years later. And the right answer when I am single might not be the right answer if I marry and have children. As I keep asking this one essential question, there might be several right answers I have to give during my life. That is why some Christians have taken early retirement in order to become missionaries. Not only do they have more to offer because of all the skills and experience they gained in their working life, but they are able to use their superannuation to fund themselves—which means that those who send them and those to whom they go have more money to spend on other important projects.

This leads me to a second "Yes, but ..." Yes, there are many right answers—so it is not the case (as I once thought) that we all should be missionaries or at least church-workers. But there should most definitely be more missionaries and church-workers—lots more! Large areas of the increasingly godless western world need to be re-evangelized, and a task of that size is going to require a great many new workers. That is also true throughout the two-thirds world, where there is such great need for the progress of the gospel and the growth of God's church. Since the potential harvest is so great but the workers are so few (Matt 9:37; Luke 10:2), that suggests that some of us are holding back from giving the right answer, or at least the best answer, to the one essential question. Could this be the right moment for you to think again about how you can make your life count most for the honour of the Lord Jesus?

Perhaps you reached that point some time ago, and so you read the book to test your suitability or readiness for serving in a ministry position. Whatever conclusion you have reached, it's a good idea to talk this through with a wise Christian friend who knows you and also knows something about Christian ministry, to work out what your next step should be. But if you haven't been able to reach a conclusion, you might find it helpful to draw up a balance-sheet of all of the pros and cons you are now aware of. Just doing so might be enough to point you in the right direction—but whatever the outcome, it would be worth talking all of this through with that wise Christian friend.

If you read the book because you are struggling in your ministry, I hope that it has helped you to work out why you are having a difficult time, and also that it has given you real encouragement to persevere. I

175

hope in particular that it has given you a clearer and bigger grasp of what Christian ministry involves, so that you can see how important it is and what an immense privilege it is. But it is never a good idea to try and struggle through on your own—so I hope you will go to talk and pray about the problems you have been having with someone you can trust to keep confidences and who will keep praying for you and encouraging you. You might also get some help and encouragement from reading one or two of the books in the Bibliography that follows.

I think the various steps I have suggested will prove helpful—but by far the most important thing you can do now is to talk to God about what you have learned and about what you think you should do next. Ask him to use what you now know about Christian ministry to make you better able to serve others where you are. Ask him to keep growing and changing you so that your serving will become steadily more faithful and more fruitful. Ask him to make you more and more content to be a servant—and to be willing to serve him in new ways or new places, if that will bring him greater honour. But above all, thank him every day for the truly stunning grace in what Jesus our Servant-Lord has done to serve and save you, and for the wonderful privilege of being his servant. And keep serving!

CHRISTIAN MINISTRY: A BIBLIOGRAPHY

Your Bible is the only infallible book you will ever read. So you should not expect the books on this list to get everything right—any more than this one has. The reason I have included them is that each of these books has good things to say about Christian ministry. They won't all be equally relevant for you at this point, but it is helpful for you to know that they are there for when you might need them.

I am sure that these are not the only good books on this subject—but at some point, you have to stop reading about Christian ministry and just get on with it! So this bibliography lists only books that I have read and found worthwhile, and the fact that a book is not included here is not necessarily my way of saying "not worth reading" (although I have read some that fall into that category!).

I have deliberately begun with books that come from earlier times, just to remind us that believers in the past knew a thing or two! But while there is much we can learn from them, we must not try to copy them, for they served in a very different world from ours.

Section A: Gems from the Past

Richard Baxter   The Reformed Pastor (Banner of Truth, 1974 [1656])

Martin Bucer   Concerning the True Care of Souls (Banner of Truth, 2009 [1538])

John Calvin   Sermons on Titus (Banner of Truth, 2015 [1561])

Those who can read English as it was spelt and printed in 1579, will get great benefit from the first translation of Calvin's Sermons on the Epistles to Timothy and Titus, published in facsimile by Banner of Truth in 1983.

Larry J Michael   Spurgeon on Leadership: Key Insights for Christian Leaders from the Prince of Preachers, revised (Kregel, 2010)

Steve Miller   C.H. Spurgeon on Spiritual Leadership (Moody, 2003)

CH Spurgeon   Lectures to My Students (Hendrickson, 2010 [1875])

Section B: Good Stuff from our own Time

Christopher Ash   Zeal Without Burnout: Seven Keys to a Lifelong Ministry of Sustainable Sacrifice (Good Book, 2016)

Barbara Bancroft   Running On Empty: The Gospel for Women in Ministry (New Growth, 2014)

Paul Barnett   Paul—A Pastor's Heart in Second Corinthians (Aquila, 2012)

Richard Bewes   Equipped to Serve (Christian Focus, 2013)

Peter Brain   Going the Distance: How to Stay Fit for a Lifetime of Ministry (Matthias, 2004)

DA Carson   The Cross and Christian Ministry: Leadership Lessons from 1 Corinthians (Baker, 2004)

Alan E Craddock   Driven to Despair: Perfectionism and Ministry (Mosaic, 2013)

Brian Croft   The Pastor's Ministry: Biblical Priorities for Faithful Shepherds (Zondervan, 2015)

Mark Dever   Discipling: How to Help Others Follow Jesus (Crossway, 2016)

Mark Dever & Paul Alexander   The Deliberate Church: Building Your Ministry on the Gospel (Crossway, 2005)

Reid Ferguson   The Little Book of Things You Should Know About Ministry (Christian Focus, 2002)

Ajith Fernando   The Family Life of a Christian Leader (Crossway, 2016)

Jonathan Griffiths   The Ministry Medical: A Health-Check from 2 Timothy (Christian Focus, 2013)

Craig Hamilton   Wisdom in Leadership: The How and Why of Leading the People You Serve (Matthias Media, 2015)

John Hindley   Serving Without Sinking: How to Serve Christ and Keep Your Joy (Good Book, 2013)

Marcus Honeysett   Fruitful Leaders: How to Make, Grow, Love and Keep Them (IVP, 2011)

Kent & Barbara Hughes	Liberating Ministry from the Success Syndrome (Tyndale House, 1987)
Timothy Keller	Shaped by the Gospel: Doing Balanced, Gospel-Centered Ministry in Your City (Zondervan, 2016)
Dave Kraft	Mistakes Leaders Make (Crossway, 2012)
Jonathan Lamb	Integrity: Leading with God Watching (IVP, 2006)
Jonathan Lunde	Following Jesus, The Servant King: A Biblical Theology of Covenantal Discipleship (Zondervan, 2010)
Paul Mallard	Staying Fresh: Serving with Joy (IVP, 2015)
Colin Marshall & Tony Payne	The Trellis and the Vine: The Ministry Mind-Set that Changes Everything (Matthias, 2009)
Colin Marshall & Tony Payne	The Vine Project: Shaping Your Ministry-Culture Around Disciple-Making (Matthias Media, 2016)
Kyle McClellan	Mea Culpa: Learning from Mistakes in the Ministry (Christian Focus, 2015)
John Piper	Brothers, We Are Not Professionals: A Plea to Pastors for Radical Ministry, updated and expanded edition (B&H, 2013)
Jeramie Rinne	Church Elders: How to Shepherd God's People Like Jesus (Crossway, 2014)
David I Starling	UnCorinthian Leadership: Thematic Reflections on 1 Corinthians (Cascade, 2014)
John Stott	Calling Christian Leaders: Biblical Models of Church, Gospel and Ministry (IVP, 2002)
James Taylor	Pastors Under Pressure: Conflicts on the Outside, Fears Within, 2nd ed. (DayOne, 2004)
William Taylor & David Dargue	Style or Substance? The Nature of True Christian Ministry (Christian Focus, 2016)
Derek Tidball	Builders and Fools: Leadership the Bible Way (IVP, 1999)

Derek Tidball	Ministry by the Book: New Testament Patterns for Pastoral Leadership (IVP, 2008)
Steve Timmis	Gospel-Centred Leadership: Becoming the Servant God Wants You to Be (Good Book, 2012)
Paul David Tripp	Dangerous Calling: The Unique Challenges of Pastoral Ministry (IVP, 2012)
Jared C Wilson	The Pastor's Justification: Applying the Work of Christ in Your Life and Ministry (Crossway, 2013)

And finally, a witty send-up which will teach you how not to do Christian ministry:

Rev'd Gerald Ambulance, My Ministry Manual (SPCK, 2002)

If you have enjoyed this book, you might like to consider:

- supporting the work of the Latimer Trust
- reading more of our publications
- recommending them to others

See www.latimertrust.org for more information.

LATIMER PUBLICATIONS

LS80	Were they Preaching 'Another Gospel'? Justification by faith in the Second Century	Andrew Daunton-Fear
LS81	Thinking Aloud: Responding to the Contemporary Debate about Marriage, Sexuality and Reconciliation	Martin Davie
LS82	Spells, Sorcerers and Spirits: Magic and the Occult in the Bible	Kirsten Birkett

Latimer Briefings

LB01	The Church of England: What it is, and what it stands for	R. T. Beckwith
LB02	Praying with Understanding: Explanations of Words and Passages in the Book of Common Prayer	R. T. Beckwith
LB03	The Failure of the Church of England? The Church, the Nation and the Anglican Communion	A. Pollard
LB04	Towards a Heritage Renewed	H.R.M. Craig
LB05	Christ's Gospel to the Nations: The Heart & Mind of Evangelicalism Past, Present & Future	Peter Jensen
LB06	Passion for the Gospel: Hugh Latimer (1485–1555) Then and Now. A commemorative lecture to mark the 450th anniversary of his martyrdom in Oxford	A. McGrath
LB07	Truth and Unity in Christian Fellowship	Michael Nazir-Ali
LB08	Unworthy Ministers: Donatism and Discipline Today	Mark Burkill
LB09	Witnessing to Western Muslims: A Worldview Approach to Sharing Faith	Richard Shumack
LB10	Scarf or Stole at Ordination? A Plea for the Evangelical Conscience	Andrew Atherstone
LB11	How to Write a Theology Essay	Michael P. Jensen
LB12	Preaching: A Guidebook for Beginners	Allan Chapple
LB13	Justification by Faith: Orientating the Church's teaching and practice to Christ (Toon Lecture 1)	Michael Nazir-Ali
LB14	"Remember Your Leaders": Principles and Priorities for Leaders from Hebrews 13	Wallace Benn
LB15	How the Anglican Communion came to be and where it is going	Michael Nazir-Ali
LB16	Divine Allurement: Cranmer's Comfortable Words	Ashley Null
LB17	True Devotion: In Search of Authentic Spirituality	Allan Chapple
LB18	Commemorating War and Praying for Peace: A Christian reflection on the Armed Forces	John Neal

Anglican Foundations Series

FWC	The Faith We Confess: An Exposition of the 39 Articles	Gerald Bray
AF02	The 'Very Pure Word of God': The Book of Common Prayer as a Model of Biblical Liturgy	Peter Adam
AF03	Dearly Beloved: Building God's People Through Morning and Evening Prayer	Mark Burkill
AF04	Day by Day: The Rhythm of the Bible in the Book of Common Prayer	Benjamin Sargent
AF05	The Supper: Cranmer and Communion	Nigel Scotland
AF06	A Fruitful Exhortation: A Guide to the Homilies	Gerald Bray
AF07	Instruction in the Way of the Lord: A Guide to the Prayer Book Catechism	Martin Davie
AF08	Till Death Us Do Part: "The Solemnization of Matrimony" in the Book of Common Prayer	Simon Vibert
AF09	'Sure and Certain Hope': Death and Burial in the Book of Common Prayer	Andrew Cinnamond

Latimer Books

GGC	God, Gays and the Church: Human Sexuality and Experience in Christian Thinking	eds. Lisa Nolland, Chris Sugden, Sarah Finch
WTL	The Way, the Truth and the Life: Theological Resources for a Pilgrimage to a Global Anglican Future	eds. Vinay Samuel, Chris Sugden, Sarah Finch
AEID	Anglican Evangelical Identity – Yesterday and Today	J.I.Packer, N.T.Wright
IB	The Anglican Evangelical Doctrine of Infant Baptism	John Stott, Alec Motyer
BF	Being Faithful: The Shape of Historic Anglicanism Today	Theological Resource Group of GAFCON
TPG	The True Profession of the Gospel: Augustus Toplady and Reclaiming our Reformed Foundations	Lee Gatiss
SG	Shadow Gospel: Rowan Williams and the Anglican Communion Crisis	Charles Raven
TTB	Translating the Bible: From William Tyndale to King James	Gerald Bray
PWS	Pilgrims, Warriors, and Servants: Puritan Wisdom for Today's Church	ed. Lee Gatiss
PPA	Preachers, Pastors, and Ambassadors: Puritan Wisdom for Today's Church	ed. Lee Gatiss
CWP	The Church, Women Bishops and Provision: The Integrity of Orthodox Objections to the Proposed Legislation Allowing Women Bishops	
TSF	The Truth Shall Set You Free: Global Anglicans in the 21st Century	ed. Charles Raven
LMM	*Launching Marsden's Mission: The Beginnings of the Church Missionary Society in New Zealand, viewed from New South Wales*	eds. Peter G Bolt David B. Pettett
MST1	*Listen To Him: Reading and Preaching Emmanuel in Matthew*	Ed. Peter Bolt
GWC	*The Genius of George Whitefield: Reflections on his Ministry from 21st Century Africa*	Ed. Benjamin Dean & Adriaan Neele